SHOULD I FILE: A DEFINITIVE GUIDE TO BANKRUPTCY

by

JEFFREY D. HOLST

Attorney

SHOULD I FILE:
A DEFINITIVE GUIDE TO BANKRUPTCY

Jeffrey D. Holst
Attorney

Signature Legal Publishing, LLC

FIRST EDITION   DECEMBER 2012

Signature Legal Publishing LLC
134 W. University Dr., Ste. 316
Rochester, MI 48307

ISBN-13:   978-1481248730

ISBN-10:   1481248731

For Becky

thanks for everything.

ACKNOWLEDGMENTS

There is little about writing a book that is done on one's own. Without Jason Miller's interest in this project it would be nothing more than a partially written file on my laptop. He regularly checked in with me and when I drifted to other things he pushed me back on track. And so I thank him for knowing that I could complete this book even before I knew I could.

Without my mother's help this book would be unreadable. Her donated time saved me hours of editing and her insights helped me discover the areas where my ideas were unclear. She cleaned up my grammar, placed commas when I neglected them, and removed them when I added them for no apparent reason. Any errors that remain are entirely mine. Thank you mom.

Ben and Michal Wetmore did all the hard stuff and I thank them for helping me to put this together and for dealing with my demands in a professional and competent manner. You guys rock.

I wish to thank all the other people who have helped me along the way including Brandy Skantze, Travis Bronik, Jeffrey Hampel, Dr. Clark Johnson, the many attorneys, judges, trustees and other legal professionals I have worked with, my clients who have taught me more than I have taught them, my dad because without him and his experience I would never have gotten into bankruptcy in the first place, my wife for encouraging me to finish and for giving me the time to do so, and the rest of my family. Many of you may not know that you helped me with this project but each of you contributed in your own way and I really appreciate it.

Finally I am sure that I have forgotten someone, I wish to thank everyone else. I couldn't have done it without you.

Jeffrey D. Holst , Chattanooga, December 1st 2012

CONTENTS:

THIS BOOK IS FOR YOU

This is not a do it yourself bankruptcy book. This book is for people with questions about bankruptcy. It is designed to help the reader gain a general understanding about the bankruptcy process with the hope that this understanding will alleviate some of the stress of dealing with issue. By reading this book you will gain valuable information that will help you make intelligent decisions about bankruptcy.

There are plenty of do it yourself bankruptcy books on the market. Unfortunately, these books fall short. The do it yourself books do little more than provide readers forms and instructions. This is a different type of book. It provides an outline of the process. It is full of examples taken from my experiences as an bankruptcy attorney. The examples provided are real situations, taken from the hundreds of bankruptcies with which I have been involved. I have spent a substantial amount of time observing the bankruptcy process. I have listened to the fears and concerns of my clients, and I have been there to help them through the issues that have arisen in process. Some examples are based on my experiences as a bankruptcy attorney, and on my clients, others are based on events that I have witnessed while sitting in a bankruptcy courtroom, or in a United States Trustee's office or hearing room.

Bankruptcies can go horribly wrong. When they do it is not a pleasant experience for the individuals involved. Nearly every time that there is a problem in bankruptcy, it is the result of inadequate preparation. It could be that the attorney involved did not ask the right questions; it could be that the debtor provided inaccurate or incomplete answers to the questions that were asked by the attorney; it also could be that the debtor or the debtor's attorney failed to appreciate the consequences of the decisions they were making. But in each of these cases a little preparation and a better understanding of the law could have greatly reduced the cost to the debtor. Ultimately, it is the debtor that bares the costs of errors.

The good news is that all or at least most of the problems that could arise in bankruptcy are avoidable. If the debtor and the debtor's attorney are prepared and well informed about the law and the about the debtor's financial position, there is no reason for the process to be problematic.

It is important to remember that this book is not a substitute for legal advice and is not intended to form an attorney client relationship between us. This book is instead intended to help you begin the process of understanding bankruptcy. By building this initial understanding, you will be better equipped to make the right choices concerning bankruptcy. Reading this book should also point you in the right direction. It should give you the insight necessary to hire high quality legal counsel.

There are many good bankruptcy attorneys, but also many attorneys who file bankruptcies without the benefit of a good understanding of bankruptcy and how it works. It is for this reason that you need to be informed. You need to understand the critical issues involved so that when you interview an attorney, you can make sure that you get one who is well-prepared.

I congratulate you for making the decision to educate yourself about bankruptcy. By taking this step, you have indicated a willingness to take this process seriously, and as wise man once told me, "That's better than not so much."

INTRODUCTION

Having difficulty with your debt load is not unusual in this day and age, in fact, for most people it's a way of life. However, it doesn't have to be that way. You may have heard that there have been changes to the bankruptcy law that make it more difficult or even impossible to file and to clear up your debts. This is simply not true; in fact the total number of filers has risen for several years in row. In reality, the changes to the Bankruptcy Code were designed to prevent people from cheating and stealing. They were designed to prevent people from borrowing money that they never intended to pay and then using the bankruptcy law to get away with it.

If you are a generally honest person, a person who intends or intended to pay their debts but now find yourself in a situation that make paying your debts difficult or even impossible then you should consider bankruptcy and I congratulate you for buying this book. In this book you will learn whether bankruptcy is right for you. By reading this book you are preparing yourself for what might come and you are learning to use the law to protect you from creditors who may not care about you and would otherwise do anything including garnishing you wages (taking food off you table), seizing your property (taking your vehicle even if it prevents you from getting to and from work), or even cleaning out your bank accounts making so you can't pay your rent or your mortgage. It important that you understand that the debt collectors that you are dealing with or will be dealing with may sound nice, they may even care about you on some level, but at the end of the day their job is or will be to take your money. And the only way that they get paid is by taking your money from you. Fortunately the United States Bankruptcy Code is designed to help people out of situations just like yours. This book will help you understand if you can qualify for bankruptcy (you can), if you should file for bankruptcy (depends on your situation) and finally what you can and should do now to improve your financial situation and in turn your life.

A quick note on this book, its format, it author and how to get the most from reading this book. The book is primarily the product of my personal experiences as a bankruptcy professional. I have been academically trained in the law, and, unlike many attorneys, I have taken graduate level classes focusing exclusively on bankruptcy. After law school, I continued to study the area of bankruptcy going to conferences and seminars. I also met with and discussed bankruptcy with attorneys who had been practicing for years in the field and who had filed literally thousands of bankruptcies. This base of education and professional experience allowed me to successfully file hundreds of bankruptcies and successfully discharge (eliminate) millions and millions of dollars in debt using the Bankruptcy Code as it was intended. I have included personal observations where appropriate and have also included case studies based upon real clients that I have worked with. In all cases, I have removed all identifying information about my clients and in some cases, I may have combined one or more individuals to clarify the under lying issue highlighted by that particular case study. Much of the information in this book comes directly from my experience as a bankruptcy professional and as an attorney. The rest of it comes from the sources as indicated or from general observations that I have made.

A Final Note on This Book

All cases and personal situations are different and are dependent on the facts and particular circumstances. Nothing in this book should be construed as legal advice. Please seek out high quality professional advice about the particulars of your financial situation before undertaking any type of bankruptcy.

THINGS TO KEEP IN MIND WHEN READING THIS BOOK

There are many different types of bankruptcies. The most commonly understood form of bankruptcy is known as a Chapter 7 bankruptcy; it is also called Liquidation or total bankruptcy. Throughout this book I will refer to it as Chapter 7. I will also refer to Chapter 13 bankruptcies, which are often called a repayment or restructuring bankruptcy.

These names are derived from a section of the United States Federal Code specifically 11 USC Chapter 7 and 11 USC Chapter 13. There are several other types of bankruptcy that are outside the purview of this writing. They generally involve complex business restructuring or specific entities like the Chapter 9, which is for cities and states or the Chapter 12, which is for certain farm restructuring programs.

This book will cover Chapter 7 and Chapter 13 in considerable detail. At this point all you really need to know is that a Chapter 7 allows the debtor to eliminate most debts and keep most of his stuff without making any kind of payments to the Trustee. And that in a Chapter 13 the debtor enters into a plan to repay some part of her debts. After a period of time, typically between 36 and 60 months, any remaining dischargeable debt that they have is discharged.

Make sure that you understand this difference before moving on. As I said these two types will be covered in greater detail as you move through the book, but a basic understanding will make this process much easier.

Chapter 7: Most common type of bankruptcy available for business and for individuals. In most cases individuals who file this chapter can keep all of their assets and are not required to pay any of their debts, it is for this reason it is sometimes also referred to as "Total bankruptcy."

Chapter 13: Is a type of bankruptcy only available to real people (businesses cannot file this type). It is a repayment plan bankruptcy that last between 3 years and 5 years, with the debtor typically paying monthly or weekly payments. At the conclusion of the 3-5 year period, any remaining debt can be discharged.

These definitions and many others appear in the glossary at the back of this book. As you read this book it may be helpful to refer to the glossary; this tool can help to ensure that you understand the vocabulary used in this book. Understanding the terminology is critical to understanding the bankruptcy process.

MYTHS AND MISCONCEPTIONS

Before you dig in too far, I think it may be useful to discover the top ten myths and misconceptions people, like you, have about bankruptcy. This section outlines these myths and mtisconceptions quickly, but most will be covered in detail later in the book. While the list may not include every misunderstood aspect of bankruptcy, it is compiled from my experience talking to hundreds or perhaps thousands of people about bankruptcy. There are two important reasons for this section. The first is to give you, the reader, a preview of the material covered later in this book. The second, and perhaps more important reason, is to make sure that early on in this discussion you recognize that the confusion you have or are experiencing about this often difficult subject is normal. Almost every person with whom I have met with and discussed bankruptcy or debt related issues has had some misconceptions about the process. These myths and misconceptions are the most common that I have heard and by getting past these myths you can be assured that you make an intelligent and reasoned decision about your financial future.

Myth #1: Only Losers File for Bankruptcy

This is perhaps the biggest myth and is probably the most common belief among the general public. The reality is that millions of people file every year. Many of these people are doctors, lawyers and other professionals. Many are normal regular hardworking individuals. In many cases a person is forced to file due to things completely out of their control.

Myth #2: People Who File for Bankruptcy Lose Everything They Have

Almost every day in my practice I heard somebody say, "I really don't want to file because I need my car to get back and forth to work," or "I need your help but I can't file bankruptcy because I can't afford to lose my home, it would devastate my children." My experience is that even many attorneys believe this one as well.

The good news is that you don't have to lose your house, cars, furniture, collectibles, photo albums, jewelry, or even your dog. In most cases, my clients have been able keep everything. Obviously there are limits to what a person can keep in bankruptcy, but for most people these limits are quite generous. This is covered in much more detail later on in this book in the section entitled "What Can I Keep?"

Myth #3: If I File My Credit Will Be Destroyed Forever

Most people believe this one. My experience is that even many attorneys even believe this one. However it is simply not true. First of all, the Fair Credit Reporting Act specifically limits the time frame in which a bankruptcy appears on your credit report to ten years. This means that ten years and one day after your discharge, the bankruptcy will no longer have any effect on your credit. The additional good news is that there is no need to wait that long. Many people with whom I have worked have gotten credit cards and even mortgages with a year or less after filing for bankruptcy. How this works and what you should do to rebuild your credit will be covered later in the section entitled "OK I filed, What do I do Now?"

Myth #4: If I File All My Friends Will Find Out

For some reason this myth just will not go away. Lots and lots of people whom I have dealt with have expressed fear and anxiety over people finding out that they filed. And while this issue is discussed in much greater detail a little later on, it is important for you to know that in many cases, in fact, in most cases, the only people that ever find out about your bankruptcy are those people you have told about it. This myth is covered more fully in the section entitled "Everyone is Doing it Maybe You Should Too."

Myth #5: If I File It Will Be Harder to Get or Keep a Job

The good news is that there are strict rules in the Code that prevent this type of discrimination. Just like it's illegal not to hire someone based on race or religion it is also illegal to discriminate against someone in the hiring process based on a past bankruptcy filing. We will deal with this issue and many similar issues in greater detail in the section entitled "It's Not as Bad as You Think."

Myth #6: You can't Get Rid of Medical or Tax Debts

In general, most types of debt are dischargeable, meaning that you can get rid of them. There are virtually no exceptions to this rule that results in preventing a person from discharging medical bills or medical debts. Taxes are a bit trickier for sure but also can be discharged in the right circumstances. This topic will be more fully dealt with in the section entitled "What's a Discharge and How does it Work?"

Myth #7: I Should Max Out My Credit Cards Because When I File I Won't Have to Pay Anyway

Not so fast...This one is a big no-no. Don't do it, its fraud, it's stealing and it just ain't right. Seriously if your cards are maxed already OK, you can deal with that, but don't ever charge something or borrow money with the intent not to pay it back. It is criminal and you will not get away with it. There are strict rules that prevent this type of behavior. Learn about this and couple of other things you should avoid in the section entitled "What can go Wrong and How to Avoid it."

Myth #8: I don't Owe Enough, or I Owe Too Much to File Bankruptcy

The simple fact is that there are no limits to the minimum and maximum amounts of debt a person can have and still file for bankruptcy. Technically a person could file if they owed only one dollar, but of course this would be a bad idea when you consider the costs involved.

In reality, peoples' circumstances are different and while a person making $100,000 dollars a year or more wouldn't usually file over five to ten thousand dollars of debt, a person on a fixed income taking home less than $12,000 dollars a year almost certainly would have no other choice. It is all relative, and recognizing this, the Congress has not placed absolute limits on debt amounts in the Code. (There are a couple of technical exceptions for very high debt amounts, but even in those circumstances they don't prevent filing out right, they just effect the debtor's eligibility for particular chapters of the code).

Myth #9: I Make Too Much or Too Little to File for Bankruptcy

This myth is similar to the last one; it is relative to personal circumstances. However, the bankruptcy Abuse Prevention and Consumer Protection Act of 2005 places some limits on income that can in some circumstances, prevent high income people from selecting to file a Chapter 7 bankruptcy, but nothing precludes them from filing another form of bankruptcy such as a Chapter 13 bankruptcy. For a closer look at the bankruptcy Abuse and Consumer Protection Act, see the section entitled a "Brief History of Bankruptcy." The issue of chapter selection will be looked at more fully, in the section entitled: "Types of Bankruptcies/Choosing the Right One for You."

Myth #10: If I File It Will Destroy My Husband or Wife's Credit

Nope, nothing in the Bankruptcy Code requires a person to file with their spouse, or even tell their spouse that they are filing. As we well know not all people are 100% truthful with their spouses about their financial situation. I have had this issue come up at least a couple of times a year since I started doing bankruptcy work. The truth is that it is possible to file without telling your spouse and, in fact, assuming that they don't pay much attention to your finances you probably will be able to prevent them from ever knowing about it.

However I don't recommend it. In my practice I wouldn't do it. I know some attorneys who have done this type of thing but, in my opinion, it is really not a good idea. That being said, I often have filed for one spouse or the other so that they can eliminate all or most of their debt and yet still have one person in the relationship with really good credit. This technique can be quite useful in certain circumstances. The particulars of this are a bit advanced for this book. I would suggest that you consult a good bankruptcy attorney who is well trained and familiar with the law before considering this type of individual filing.

The general rule is: if you don't file, it doesn't affect your credit. This means there will be no negative hit to the credit report of the the non-filing spouse, but it also means that in the case of joint debts, the non-filing spouse remains liable for the entire jointly owed obligation.

A BRIEF HISTORY OF BANKRUPTCY

Before the modern era there was no official bankruptcy law. In many cases, failure to pay your debts resulted in debtor's prison, slavery or even death. Even after the idea of bankruptcy came about the consequence of bankruptcy was often imprisonment or death. Genghis Kahn, for example, is said to have included a provision in his bankruptcy law that mandated the death penalty to anyone who became bankrupt three times. And while it may seem that the modern consequences of bankruptcy are bad, you can be assured that they will not include death.

Many of the world's major religions have mechanisms built in to alleviate or even eliminate debt. These mechanisms are found in the Bible, the Torah, and the Qur'an. The Torah and the Old Testament included a year of Jubilee when most or all debts were forgiven. This concept forms the basis of modern day Chapter 7 bankruptcy where the debtor's debts are forgiven often completely.

The second chapter of the Qur'an (Sura Al-Baqara) Verse 280 states that "...if someone is in hardship, then let there be postponement until a time of ease." This statement resembles modern day Chapter 13 bankruptcy where debtors propose a plan to repay their debts on a schedule that it more affordable than the current schedule.

Modern bankruptcy first leapt on to the scene in Britain with the bankruptcy act of 1542 (34 and 35, Henry VIII, c.4). In the United States of the first acts of the Federal Government was to create bankruptcy protection. In fact, the power to regulate bankruptcy in the United States was granted by the Constitution when it was ratified in 1789. In Article I, Section 8, Clause 4,

Congress was granted the power to legislate "uniform laws on the subject of bankruptcies" throughout the several States. The very first act of Congress was the bankruptcy Act of 1800, and while that act was repealed and amend multiple times before the current law was enacted in 1938 the basic concept remains very much the same. There been several changes to the bankruptcy laws since 1938, but in general the law remains the same.

Many readers will recall the Bankruptcy Abuse Prevention and Consumer Protection Act of 2005. When the bill passed in to law the news media, fueled by bankruptcy attorneys looking for a quick buck, made it sound as if once the law took effect in October of 2005 it would become nearly impossible to file a bankruptcy. And if you were successful in qualifying ,you would still spend many years in debt and in many cases would lose all of your personal property. After the law passed and was signed into law in April of 2005 by then President George W. Bush, these claims were repeated so often that many of them persist today.

Most aspects of the new law did not take effect until October and the period of time between April and October of 2005 became a virtual gold rush for bankruptcy attorneys many of whom filed more than ten times their usual number of bankruptcy. One such attorney I talked to told me that he filed over 400 bankruptcies in the five days before the law took effect. This mad rush of filings was most likely due to the misconception that after October of 2005 bankruptcy as we know it would no longer exist. Ironically, many of the attorneys practicing in this area fell for their own hype. I know of several former bankruptcy attorneys so scared of the new law that they stopped filing them all together.

In retrospect, the changes in the bankruptcy law did little to prevent the protection of the code. The most significant change from the average debtors perspective is the creation of an income based test, known as the means test. The means test prevents certain high income debtors from discharging (eliminating) all of their debt. In the case of high income debtors or debtors who make more than the means test allowable amounts (which varies by state) there is a requirement that make their best efforts to pay back some portion of their debts. The amount that they pay back is determined by, among other things, their ability to pay after allowances for reasonable living expenses. This type of repayment bankruptcy is known as a Chapter 13 bankruptcy.

EVERYONE IS DOING IT
MAYBE YOU SHOULD TOO

In spite of all these changes the raw number of bankruptcy files has continued to increase. The only exception to this trend occurred in numbers for 2011 which may be an encouraging sign for the future but offers little comfort to the millions of people who are forced by their circumstances to file each year.

Total bankruptcy Filings in U.S.

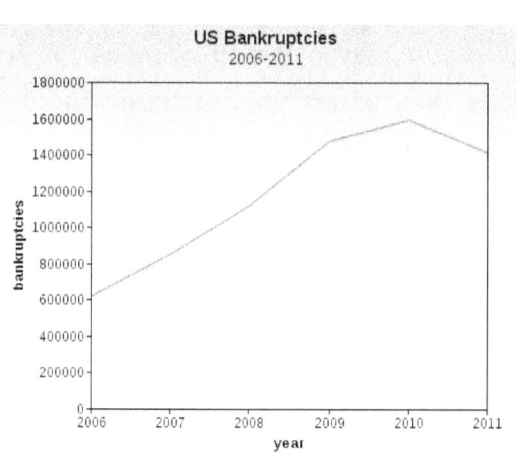

Year	2011	2010	2009	2008	2007	2006
Business	47,806	56,282	60,837	43,533	28,322	19,695
Non-Business	1,362,847	1,536,799	1,412,838	1,074,108	822,590	597,965
Total	1,410,653	1,593,081	1,473,675	1,117,641	850,912	617,660

One thing to keep in mind with these numbers is that they represent fillings only and the total number of people who filed is actually somewhat higher since husbands and wives almost always file joint cases and as such would only count as one filing for the two people. The real number of people who filed bankruptcy in the last six years, the six years immediately following the bankruptcy Abuse Prevention and Consumer Protection Act of 2005 (BAPCPA) is probably close to 10 million people. Because of rules limiting the frequency of filing nearly all of these people will not have filed more than once in this time period. This means that it is very likely that more than 10 million different people have filled bankruptcy under the new bankruptcy law. At this rate, you can infer that as many as 15-17 million individuals have filed and gone through some form of bankruptcy in a ten year period starting in 2006. With official estimates of the total adult population (aged 21 and over) at 217,202,821in 2008, somewhere between 1 in 10 and 1 in 15 people will have filed for bankruptcy during that period.

So look around you, you may not know it but many of your friends and possibly even your family members have filed or will file. The same can be said for you -- if you decide to file for bankruptcy, most likely your friends and family will never know, and if they do, the reason that they find out will almost certainly be because you told them about it. My personal experience counseling hundreds of people about bankruptcy is that one of the major hang ups that people have is that they are embarrassed or afraid that someone might find out about their circumstance.

Case Study #1: Martin and Rebecca

Martin and Rebecca are both public school teachers, they make good money and only work nine months a year. Their jobs are hard and notable. They are by all standards excellent teachers and are extremely well liked in their community. Martin coaches several sports at the high school where he teaches and Rebecca spends summers going to Martin's games and practices. She also goes to their vacation home on a lake and writes. Her first book was picked up by a minor publisher and a sold a few thousand copies mostly in her local community to people who support Martin's and her schools. She continues to write, hoping that one day one of her novels will make it big and dig them out of the hell in which they live.

Wait a minute, hell? It sounds like heaven! They have their dream jobs and a vacation home on a lake. But appearances can be deceiving, can't they. Let's take a closer look. By the time they came in to my office, they had almost given up. Whether it was pride or sheer personal fortitude they had put off that first meeting way too long. Their debts were spiraling out of control; they had fallen for a debt restructuring scheme that had them paying over $1,000 a month in to a fund that was supposed to settle their outstanding credit card debts. Now two years later, they were getting phone calls 15-20 times an hour and were so embarrassed that they turned their phones off when in public and even turned their ringers off while people were visiting their home. When they started the "restructuring plan," they were told it would take about 18-20 months until all their debts would be satisfied. They were instructed to stop paying all credit cards and pay the money instead to this company, who, for a small fee, would negotiate away their debts and pay the settlements with a fund that they created from the $1,000 monthly payments.

This plan sounded great to Martin and Rebecca who had been struggling with debt after building up some fifty thousand dollars in credit card debt. (I know it sounds shocking but it happens to smart people all the time). So how much did they owe two years after paying $1,000 per month? Most people would guess that their debts were settled or at the very least greatly reduced. Guess again. $87,000, after 24 payments of $1,000 their debt of $50,000 had grown by $37,000. When they got their annual statement the second year and saw this figure, they were understandably shocked. When Martin called the company and inquired as to what was going on, he was told that it was all part of the process and that over the last two years a fund had been created and once the credit card companies got really desperate they would settle for far less. This sounded okay to him, but fortunately as he was about to hang up he thought of one more question - how much had the settlement fund grown after 24 months? He asked and was told that the fund was currently at only $ 3,313.12!

The company had charged $1,000 up front (the first payment) and $450 a month for their "service" and after 18 months the term of the deal rolled over and they charged another 1000 "renewal fee" and the monthly fees were increased to $650 a month. These fees and several other questionable fees ended consuming almost all of the $24,000 paid in over the two year period.

After all that, it wasn't until a good friend mentioned that he had filed for bankruptcy a year or so earlier that they came to see me. The first question Martin asked me, even before telling me anything about his situation, was how did I keep his friend's bankruptcy from being public? The answer I gave him is "I didn't." The real reason he didn't know about his friend's previous filing was that in almost all cases it's simply not newsworthy. As pointed out above, millions of people file every year and for the vast majority of those cases, while it is technically a matter of the public record, nobody pays any attention. There is nothing to be gained by paying attention to bankruptcy filings. Even as a bankruptcy attorney I am reasonably certain that my best friend could file bankruptcy and keep it from me by simply not mentioning it. Generally speaking, the only time someone will find out you filed is if you tell them, or if they happen to run into you at your one and only creditors meeting, and if they do that it's either because they are also filing also or because you invited them to watch.

IT'S NOT AS BAD AS YOU THINK

As I pointed out in the last section many people, even people that you know, have filed bankruptcy successfully and without advertising it to the public and in doing so they have avoided the embarrassment or destructive effect to their personal lives that they may have otherwise experienced. If you are like many of my clients you are wondering about the effect that bankruptcy has on your business or financial life. I can almost hear you saying "sure I can file but if I do, I will lose all my possessions and my credit will be destroyed. I won't have any money or any possessions and because of my credit I won't even be able to finance for new things. I'll probably be homeless and won't even have the credit to get an apartment. Not to mention the fact that next time I apply for a job they might run a credit check and find out about my bankruptcy filing, and when they do they won't hire me."

Fortunately bankruptcy isn't as bad as many people believe. There is an absolute limit of 10 years that a bankruptcy can show up on your credit report. After that you are 100% in the clear. Of course ten years is a really long time. The good news is that it doesn't have to take that long for your credit to be repaired to the point where you can once again borrow money to buy a car a home or even to get a credit card. Strategic use of credit after filing for bankruptcy can greatly improve your credit rating. A more detailed description of this process can be found in the section entitled "OK, I Filed Now What Do I Do" towards the end of this book.

When thinking about credit most people think only of their credit score, which is an important element of one's credit.

However it is only one of several critical components that make up a person's total creditworthiness. If you think about this, it becomes very clear that this is true. If banks, or lenders of any sort only cared about credit score how long would a loan application be? My guess is that it would include a blank for your name, your date of birth, your social security number, and your address. After all, that's the only information that they need to pull your credit score. If you have filled out a loan application in the last two to three decades you know that they ask many more questions than that. Below I have included the typical questions found on a generic loan application (in abbreviated form) so that we can better understand the underlying purpose behind the questions asked. By doing so you can get a more complete picture of the lending process and how lending institutions decide on your individual creditworthiness.

PERSONAL DETAILS
Name of applicant
      First name (s)_____
      Middle name_____
      Surname_____
Date of Birth: Day _____ Month _____Year _____
Marital Status: Married_____ Single_____ Divorced _____
Social Security Number _____

EMPLOYMENT AND INCOME DETAILS
(Check all that apply)
Employed full time   _____   Annual Salary _____
Employed part time   _____   Annual Salary_____
Self employed   _____   Annual Income_____
Unemployed   _____
Address of employer/ business_____
Business Telephone Number_____

Other Income (identify all sources and amounts)
      Gross annual income_____
      Income after tax_____

Liabilities (List all debts including money owed to family members)
House   _____   Amount owed _____
Credit Cards   _____   Amount owed _____
    _____   Amount owed _____
    _____   Amount owed _____
    _____   Amount owed _____

Other Liabilities_____   Amount owed _____
    _____   Amount owed _____

CONTACT INFORMATION
      Street Address_____
      City_____
      State_____
      Telephone_____

Many forms will require even more information but the above form is a typical credit card application. Notice that there are three broad categories of information that the lender is seeking. First, personal identification information, this is to determine your credit score; second, information about your income and finally, information about your debts. Notice that they do not ask if you filed a bankruptcy in the past, so if it doesn't show on your credit report, (i.e. it has been more than 10 years) then it no longer even factors in to this equation. I will address how to rebuild your credit after a bankruptcy towards the end of this book.

The second grouping of information that is always asked on a credit application is how much money do you make? The reason for this seems relatively clear. They want to make sure that you make enough money to be able to afford the payments on the loan you are applying for. It really doesn't matter how high your credit score is if you don't make enough money to make the required minimum payments. Failure to have properly assessed the individual's ability to pay is one of the major components of the sub-prime mortgage meltdown of the last few years. Lenders became quite relaxed in their income requirements and made loans to people who could not afford them.

Case Study #2: William

William was only 22 years old when he walked in to my office and he owed over $49,000 in credit card debt and had a car loan for $15,000. Unfortunately the car he was paying for was wrecked during a time period when he had inadvertently let the comprehensive insurance upon it lapse. While he said it was accidental, my guess is he simply could not afford to make the payments. It is pretty unusual for someone 22 years old to walk in to my office with nearly sixty-five thousand dollars in debt and when it does happen it's almost always the result of heavy medical cost during a period with inadequate health insurance. In William's case, he had just made some really bad choices. He had spent about fifteen thousand dollars a year more than he had made for the last four years. Spending more than one makes is not an uncommon problem in this age group but usually they simply don't have the ability to borrow that much money and when they do it is because they have a co-signer or a relatively high income.

William had neither; he worked the third shift at a gas station for minimum wage about 20 hours a week. When he told me this I immediately could see how it was that he spent more than he made. The harsh reality of his life was that he didn't make enough to support himself, especially since he had to pay about $75.00 every two weeks in child support for his three-year old son.

William is a pretty good guy. He loves his son, he works as many hours as his employer will give him, but he is uneducated and simply couldn't find a better job. Obviously William needed to file for bankruptcy and I helped him with that.

The real issue is: why was he able to borrow far more than he could ever possibly pay back? The answer is that when the economy was booming from 2002-2004 banks were making poor decisions as well. They were checking incomes and were letting the money flow. Fortunately in the last few years banks have scaled this kind of predatory lending back, but it does still happen or perhaps you borrowed in the past and still haven't found the way out.

When you think about it, it's pretty clear that income matters. I don't know what William's credit score was when he was filling out those applications, but my guess is that it was fairly high. The problem is that high credit score and low income offset each other. Low income means that a person simply can't pay a high payment. This is true in every instance. A person earning $300,000 a year may easily be able to handle a payment of three or even four thousand dollars a month, but I doubt that they could ever pay off a loan of ten million dollars or more even if they had a 780 credit score.

The third category on every loan application asks about current liabilities, in other words, how much you owe. If William had walked in to a bank while he owed over sixty thousand dollars and was making around ten thousand dollars a year, the lender would have had to be a bit crazy to offer him the loan. After all at that point there really was no realistic chance of him digging himself out from underneath his already excessive debt. However, assuming he was current on his payments and had a little credit to spare his credit score might not have been that bad. It could have even been quite good. If it wasn't good it's hard to see how he got the credit lines he was using in the first place. But if they only checked his score and his income, then the lenders might have taken a chance on him and may have given him a credit card for a few thousand dollars. One thing is certain: if they did approve William, they weren't going to get their money back from him.

It is the balance between these three things that make up the true picture of individual creditworthiness. When a lender evaluates a person's credit, they do look at the score, but they also look at the ratio of debt to income.

Debt to Income Ratio = Total Debt/ Total Income

The lower the product of this formula, the better your overall financial position is. For example if you owe $1,000 and make $100,000 dollars a year then your debt to income ratio would be calculated in the following manner.

Example #1: Debt to Income Ratio = $1,000/$10,0000 = .01

This means that for this individual their total debt is 1/100th of their gross annual income or in simple terms: their gross annual income is 100 times their total debt load. This is a very manageable number regardless of how much debt or income a person has. It would not matter if the person had one million dollars in debt if their ratio was still .01; generally speaking, they could easily afford to pay their debt. Of course, in order to keep that ratio they would have to be making one hundred million dollars a year.

Example #2: Debt to Income Ratio = $50,000/$100,000 = .5

In Example # 2 the person's income remained $100,000 a very respectable income, but the total debt increased to $50,000, which caused their debt to income ratio to rise to .5. Even at this level, they probably could afford to pay their debts, but, as you can see, the higher the ratio the more difficult it becomes to pay one debts.

Now let's look back to our young friend William and see what his debt to income ratio looked like. As you may recall William owed $64,000 and made only about $10,000 per year. This would result in the following debt to income ratio calculation.

William: Debt to Income Ratio = $64,000/$10,000 = 6.4

It's very dangerous to let your debt to income ratio rise to the point where your total debt exceeds your annual income. It is probably a good idea for you to always keep this formula in mind when deciding whether to borrow any additional money.

Now that you have seen how this ratio is calculated and understand why it is important, you can see why lenders want the information that they require. Interestingly, while filing bankruptcy hurts your credit score (which is calculated primarily on past repayment of debt), it significantly improves your debt to income ratio, arguably making you a much better credit risk after bankruptcy. Let's take a look at William's debt to equity ratio immediately after bankruptcy.

His debts were on a car, which he didn't want to keep because it was wrecked, and credit card debts. After his discharge in bankruptcy he owed nothing, which resulted in a debt to income ratio of 0 which is even better in a technical sense then our first example of .01.

William's post bankruptcy:
Debt to Income Ratio = $0/$10,000 = 0

Obviously with a relatively low income and a relatively low credit score William probably would have a difficult time borrowing significant sums of money, yet that's probably a good thing since he has little ability to pay debt at his income level.

A more typical example is when an individual is considering bankruptcy and has a car that he owes $15,000 on and also has $50,000 dollars in credit card debt. In this scenario the individual has an income of $40,000 per year.

EXAMPLE # 3: Debt to Income Ratio = $65,000/$40000 = 1.63

As you can see, this person is probably struggling to make the payments with a ratio significantly above one. If the individual chooses file bankruptcy and chooses to keep the car, post bankruptcy, he would have no credit card debt but would still owe $15,000 on the car. While we haven't quite gotten to how this works for now, trust me when I say that if you keep something that has a loan on it you still have to pay for it after bankruptcy. This would leave them with $15,000 in debt on the car and no additional debts. Obviously the bankruptcy will not affect their income.

EXAMPLE #3 After BK: Debt to Income Ratio = $15,000/$40000 = .38

Once again, the bankruptcy process greatly improves their debt to income ratio making them a much better credit risk. Many banks and lenders, who understand this trend, are quite willing to extend credit to individuals shortly after they file bankruptcy.

You may have noticed that in the above examples that none of the individuals had a home mortgage. This is because the home mortgage changes the calculation dramatically. When excluding your home it is a very good idea to keep your debt to income ratio as low as possible. For a variety of reasons the numbers are a little different when a home mortgage is involved, which is why I recommend calculating your debt to income ratio both with and without your mortgage included.

Example #4 illustrates the impact of a home mortgage on this calculation. In this scenario, the individual has a home mortgage of $150,000, credit card debt of $15,000 and income of $50,000 a year

Example #4: Debt to Income Ratio = $165,000/$50,000 = 3.3

Based on the prior examples, this would appear to be an unacceptably high debt to income ratio, however when you consider the underlying facts of this scenario, it does seem as bad as its ratio implies. This discrepancy results from two factors. The first is that the mortgage expense replaces rent expenses. And the second is that the interest rate on these types of loans are quite low relative to other loans, and this interest is tax deductible.

It is quite obvious that there is still a limit to how much a debt a person should carry for home expenses. Many experts argue that housing expenses should not exceed 25 percent of an individual's income. Calculating a debt to income ratio from this formula is a bit trickier and there is no need to go through the math here. I do suggest though when considering your debt to income ratio and determining whether or not to finance a home that you look at both issues. If your non-mortgage debt to income ratio is high you should address and correct that first before taking on additional debt. On the other hand, if the ratio is acceptable then you should look at the amount of money you currently spending on rent and look at how much your housing cost will increase after purchasing the home. And finally, it is a good idea to limit your total monthly expenses to 25 percent of your total monthly income. If you use these formulas together you will likely be able to make a more sensible decision about whether or not to purchase a home.

There are many more things to consider when deciding whether or not to purchase a home. If you have additional questions in this area you should consult a professional in the field or additional texts by authors addressing real estate. However, you should never simply rely on the advice of a realtor. Many real estate professionals are quite good, but you keep in mind that they want to sell you a house, and sometimes while it might be in their best interest for you to buy a house, it may not be in your best interest.

The main point is that after bankruptcy for a variety of reasons you will be more creditworthy. Your debt to income ratio will be greatly improved and opportunities to borrow will exist.

Perhaps I may be a little too cynical, but I think there is another reason that many people report multiple credit opportunities shortly after bankruptcy. I believe that a significant reason that some banks and lenders are willing to extend relatively easy credit post bankruptcy is the prohibition in the code limiting multiple filings. In particular, a person cannot file a second Chapter 7 bankruptcy for eight years after their most recent filing, this means that lenders are less worried about the chance that you might file for bankruptcy and not pay the underlying obligation.

OK, BUT DO I QUALIFY?

I am tempted to simply say yes, you do. The reason I say this is because if you are reading this book chances are you qualify. Technically all you need to qualify is to be a permanent legal resident of the United States or a citizen of the United States. One would guess that the courts would probably not allow a person with no creditors to file successfully for bankruptcy, but I doubt many debt free people are entertaining the idea. So I would say, yes, you do qualify.

In general. a person will qualify for some form of bankruptcy, however, in the case of repeat filers, there may be limits on their ability to get a discharge and in the case of high income earners there may be limits on the availability of a Chapter 7. Perhaps a better question would be: do I qualify for a Chapter 7 bankruptcy? That question will be answered more fully in the section entitled "Types of bankruptcy/Choosing the Right One for You."

Reading the earlier brief description of the difference between a Chapter 7 and Chapter 13 Bankruptcy leads most people to believe that a Chapter 7 is a much better deal. And frankly all things being equal it often is a much better deal for the filer. However, there are cases where a person does not qualify for a discharge in a Chapter 7, and in those cases it is often a good idea to look at a Chapter 13. As with the underlying "do I qualify" question, this issue will be dealt with much more fully in the section on choosing the right type of bankruptcy.

THE MAGIC OF THE AUTOMATIC STAY

Many potential bankruptcy clients have indicated to me that the main reason that they contacted me is that debt collectors are constantly harassing them. This "harassment" can be in the form of numerous repeated phone calls, wage garnishments, threats of lawsuits, property seizure, and even personal contact. I have had some people tell me that a creditor was camping out at the end of their driveway waiting for them to come or go. This type of behavior may not technically be harassment, but this technicality offers little comfort to a person who can not go five minutes without a call from a debt collector. Often these calls are even made to the debtor's work or to members of their family.

Fortunately the filing of a bankruptcy provides nearly immediate relief from these problems. The bankruptcy code provides as an automatic injunction, known as the automatic stay. Once, filed all collection actions must stop. Since this stay is a product of federal law, it operates to stop all state level collection actions, all phone calls, all wage garnishments, all actions to create a security interest, and even stops pending or current federal lawsuits. There is virtually no limit to the breadth of this protection.

The mere fact of filing is not magic, but it can certainly seem that way to a person who has been under the assault of continual credit contact for many months. Logistically, it may take a few days before the full effects of the stay are noticed, but the effect is immediate. If a creditor garnishes or seizes any property after the exact moment of filing the debtor is able to recover this money and failure of the creditor to return the money may result in significant sanctions against the creditor. It is also possible, in some circumstances, to recover moneys taken prior to the filing. This is done through operation of the look back period. These types of recovery actions are brought as a lawsuit by the debtor inside of the bankruptcy, called an adversary proceeding. There are many other types of adversary proceedings, some of which will be addressed later in this book.

Any person, who files for or is considering filing for bankruptcy in any chapter, should consider the effect of the automatic stay on their current financial situation. Keep in mind that the automatic stay continues until the court grants specific relief from it, or until the case terminates, through either discharge or dismissal. Willful violations of the automatic stay on the part of the creditors can result in stiff penalties to the creditor. If you are exposed to any such violations it is important to speak with a competent bankruptcy professional or at the very least make sure that you have a thorough understanding effect and duration of the automatic stay. This level of understanding is beyond the scope of this writing, and as with any legal issue, it is very important to make sure that you attain the requisite knowledge either on your own or through professional advice to ensure that your interests are adequately protected.

One last thing to keep in mind is that certain multiple filers may not have the full benefit of the automatic stay. If you have previously filed in the last few years for some form of bankruptcy protection whether or not it was dismissed or carried through all the way to discharge you must carefully consider the impacts of these limitations. So if you have previously filed make sure that you understand these limits. More informa-

tion on the effect of these serial filings can be found in 11 USC §
362 which is reproduced in full in appendix B at the back of this
book.

WHAT'S A DISCHARGE AND HOW DOES IT WORK?

The USCourts website provides the following description of a discharge.

> "A bankruptcy discharge releases the debtor from personal liability for certain specified types of debts. In other words, the debtor is no longer legally required to pay any debts that are discharged. The discharge is a permanent order prohibiting the creditors of the debtor from taking any form of collection action on discharged debts, including legal action and communications with the debtor, such as telephone calls, letters, and personal contacts."[1]

While this description is accurate it can be a bit confusing. The critical component of the discharge is the release from continuing liability. This release effectively means that you no longer have a legal requirement to pay the discharged debt.

One thing to keep in mind is that a discharge does not eliminate the underlying debt. It eliminates the filer or debtor's requirement to pay the debt. This distinction can be quite critical when considering the effects of security interests, such as mortgages. Security interests and their effects on bankruptcy are further discussed in the section entitled "What Can I Keep."

Barring litigation, or another valid denial of discharge, the debtor in bankruptcy receives the discharge automatically just before termination of the case. The discharge is ordered by the court in written form and is distributed to the debtor's credi-

---

1   http://www.uscourts.gov/FederalCourts/bankruptcy/bankruptcyBasics/DischargeIn-bankruptcy.aspx as of 4/20/2012

tors and to the debtors themselves. This order also terminates the automatic stay; of course at this point the automatic stay is no longer necessary as it is effectively replaced by the discharge. Like the automatic stay the discharge prevents creditors from collecting on the debts subject to the order.

It should be noted, however, that there are certain types of debts that are not dischargeable or that are only discharged in certain circumstances. The Bankruptcy Code specifically limits the types of debts that are discharged. Many of these limits are the result of policy concerns on the part of congress. This can be most clearly seen in the provision preventing the discharge of debts for personal injury caused by the debtor's operation of a motor vehicle while the debtor was intoxicated.

Other common types of nondischargeable debts include certain taxes, unscheduled or unlisted debts, spousal and child support debts, debts that resulted from willful or malicious injury to another person (for instance, if you hit someone in the head with a bat and they sue you, bankruptcy will not solve it for you), certain debts to governmental units, loans against tax-advantaged retirement plans, (including 401K or pension loans). In many of these cases the creditor is required to petition the court to exclude the debt from the discharge, if the creditor fails to do so then the underlying debt is discharged regardless of its base dischargeability.

Some debts are technically dischargeable, but only in limited circumstances. The most notable of these is student loan debt. Student loans are very difficult to discharge and it is important that if you are considering filing to rid yourself of the burdens of student loans that you carefully consider all relevant case law and the code itself to determine if you will be able to discharge them. I would recommend getting a good bankruptcy attorney and asking about it. You should also ask whether they have personally been involved in this process (before). If they haven't or if it has been a long time since they have dealt with this issue then ask them to recommend an attorney more familiar with this area of bankruptcy law. I do not recommend you try this on your own.

I have had limited success in this area and generally advise my clients that their chance of attaining a discharge of their student loan debts is very small and may not be worth the added cost associated with filing the requisite documents with the court. In many courts discharging a student loan requires the filing of an adversary proceeding against the United States. This type of filing is beyond the scope of this book. As I indicated before it is very important that when considering this type of filing that you find an attorney, who is very familiar with this type of process.

WHAT CAN I KEEP?

If you are like most people considering bankruptcy you are extremely concerned about this issue. The good news is that the individual filing for bankruptcy can usually keep most or all of their property. There really are only two issues that need to be addressed in order for you to fully understand what you can or cannot keep upon filing for bankruptcy - security interests and exemptions.

One last piece of good news, the discussion on exceptions to your ability to keep your possessions in bankruptcy will show you that there is almost always a way to work around that exception. These options will be covered in more detail in the section entitled "Types of Bankruptcy/Choosing the Right One for You." In many cases, you may not be able to keep something in one chapter of the code, but would have little or no difficulty keeping that same property in another chapter.

So what is a security interest? A security interest in its most simple definition is an interest in a security. Of course that definition isn't really all that helpful. The easiest way to understand security interests are by example. I have listed several common places where security interests are found below.

- Mortgages
- Car loans
- In store financing
- 90 days same as cash financing
- Rent to own

The important thing to understand is that it is not the loan that is the security interest, it is the attachment to the underlying collateral that is the security interest. Many people find this concept confusing. Examining the way a mortgage works will help explain the difference between a loan and a security interest.

Most people think of a mortgage as a loan against a house, and for the lay person that is about right. But we lawyers like to make things more complicated. In our world, the world of the Uniform Commercial Code (UCC), a security interest is not a loan at all, and a mortgage is a security interest. This means that a mortgage is not a loan. At first this appears silly, but there is a real difference that is very important to understand when it comes to bankruptcy. Loans are dischargeable (meaning they go away) and security interests are not dischargeable (meaning they don't go away).

What really happens when you finance a home is you sign at least two documents, the first is a loan, or a promissory note, where you as an individual promise to pay the money you borrowed. The second is a mortgage, or a security interest, in the collateral (in this case your house). These are two very important documents. The first, the promissory note, means that you have to pay back the money (this loan is dischargeable). The second, the security interest in the house says if you don't satisfy the loan, the lender can take the house to satisfy the loan (this obligation is not dischargeable). Sometimes it helps to think of a security interest as a loan that the house owes, and since the house can't file for bankruptcy, the house still owes the money.

It is this principle that prevents people from buying a house on credit and then filing for bankruptcy to get the debt discharged, which would then result in them getting a free house. So if that was your plan, sorry, it won't work. This doesn't mean that you can't keep your home if you file it just means that if you want to keep it you will have to still pay off the promissory note.

The process is pretty simple, after filing for bankruptcy, but before the bankruptcy is finalized, you and the creditor enter into a new agreement called a reaffirmation agreement where you basically agree to keep that debt. You should use caution when signing a reaffirmation agreement, though, because once the agreement is finalized you are stuck paying the debt even if you later end up losing the home. In this scenario you may very well be sued and since you recently came out of bankruptcy your options in bankruptcy will be even more limited than they were before.

I recommend consulting with a knowledgeable professional before signing any such agreement for two reasons. The first is to ensure that you understand your options and the consequence of the agreement. The second is that the code specifically requires the court to hold a hearing on the reaffirmation if the debtor has not consulted an attorney on the document before entering it with the court. And while most judges will simply call you in and question you to make sure that you fully understand your options before approving it, this process takes time and requires you in most cases to take an extra day off work to go to court. For this reason it is often easier to consult with an attorney and have them sign off on the agreement for you.

The same general principles apply to car loans and in some cases to store credit cards. Often big box stores have you sign a security agreement for the purchases. So if you have financed appliances or furniture it would be wise to evaluate the agreements that you have signed before you file to ensure that you fully understand your obligations. Again, on this issue, there is no substitute for good advice. If you are at all unsure or confused, you would be wise to have a knowledgeable attorney look at the documents.

It is also important to consider value of the financed item. If you owe $10,000 dollars on a 1992 Ford Escort you probably shouldn't be signing a reaffirmation agreement. You would be much better off finding a different car. I realize that this can be difficult, but when dealing with these types of issues, it is important not to forget the underlying reality of the situation.

Case Study #3: William

As you may recall, our friend William had a car that was wrecked and that he still owed a significant sum of money on this car. The car was wrecked, but it was also drivable, just barely, but it was drivable. When he first came in to my office he told me that he needed to keep his car because he couldn't afford to get another one. It never ceases to surprise me how often this sort of thing happens.

Take a closer look at this situation. William owes about $15,000 on his car and in its current state its worth somewhere between $500 and $1,000. He can barely afford to pay me for my services, in fact, the only reason he can pay me is because he is about to get his tax refund. He uses his car to get back and forth to work and also uses it to pick up his son for his parenting time. He doesn't have any other money and figures it would cost him at least $1,000 to get a car he could depend on. For this reason, he explained to me that he will need to keep his car, which he figures he can afford now that he won't have to keep paying on the credit cards.

While it is possible he could afford it, I actually doubted that he could, since this would have resulted a debt to income ratio of 1.5 ($15,000/$10,000) which is still greater than I generally recommend. If he was correct and could afford the payments of $385 per month, the question becomes should he reaffirm the debt through a reaffirmation agreement.

Not in a million years. Look at what he was proposing. He proposed that he pay $15,000 plus interest at $385 per month for a car that is worth at the most $1,000. So I asked him, "What would you say if I offered to sell you my car for $50,000?" At this point in time, I was driving a three year old sedan that was worth around $10,000. Obviously, he laughed at me and said that if I did that I would taking advantage of him and it would make me a scoundrel of sorts. My next question for him was "What if I offered to sell you a car worth $1,000 for $15,000?" To that he said, "Wait a minute that's not a fair comparison to my situation because when I bought the car I got this really good deal." But in reality, the reaffirmation he was proposing was a new obligation to pay a debt that he otherwise could get out of in bankruptcy.

Surprisingly this type of reaction is common. There are a couple of things that can be done to make this situation a little better. While it probably would not have worked in William's case, I could have tried to negotiate with the credit for a lower interest rate and or a lower principle amount. In my opinion, this should be attempted for every reaffirmation regardless of the circumstances. If the creditor will lower the interest or the amount owed, the debtor should take advantage of the savings.

In William's case however it is unlikely that the creditor would have agreed to a new value of $1000 or less.

So what other options does poor William have but to keep his car which he probably does need? He can buy another car. I know you're thinking wait he doesn't have any money. Correct, he didn't have any available money when he walked in to see me. My advice to him was to save up some money and then come back and see me. I know that sounds harsh but it's really not.

There are two ways that he could do this. The first one would be to go buy a new car with the money that he had from his tax returns instead of paying me and then simply stop paying on his car and let the bank take it back. In William's state, like most states, it takes a while before a creditor can garnish your wages. Assuming that he wasn't currently being garnished, which he wasn't, and also assuming that he was current on his car payments, which he was, in his state it would take about 90 days before the creditor could come after him personally. Sure they could exercise their rights to the car sooner than that by repossessing but in order for them to act on his promissory note they would be required to file a lawsuit and then he would have a chance to reply to it and finally only after they got a judgment on the lawsuit could they come after him personally. This is because the security interest allowed them to act quickly but the note or loan papers typically do not have a similar provision in fact unless the lender took a security interest in your cash or bank accounts they wouldn't be able to take anything other than the car without first prevailing in a lawsuit and lawsuits take time.

Let's assume for a second that William was being garnished as the result of another suit. In that case, it would be difficult or even impossible for him to wait to file. The same kind of strategy applies in that circumstance as well. However he would likely get even more time with the car without making payments because of the operation the bankruptcy stay, which will be covered in "How a Case Works/What to Expect."

In either case, he could simply take the money that he was currently spending on car payments and use them to save up and buy another car or pay my fees. Most attorneys would ask for their fee first and then have the client save for the car but this isn't always the best option so make sure that you get an attorney you can trust or at the very least make sure you understand this principle before making up your mind as to which way to go.

A final note on security interests, as you may have guessed, in order to keep something that you have signed a security interest against you need to be current on the payments. There are things that you can do to catch up these payments in a Chapter 13 bankruptcy which is a repayment type bankruptcy. These techniques will be addressed more fully in the section entitled "Types of Bankruptcy/Choosing the Right One for You."

Exemptions create limits on how much stuff a person can keep when they file for bankruptcy, but much like in security interests, there are ways around these limits. This typically involves either paying the trustee some money to "buy" back the unexempted property or the filing of a Chapter 13 bankruptcy.

So finally we get to the question that every person I have ever talked to asks me. "What can I keep?" The answer is: most people can keep everything they want to keep but there are limits and these limits are a product of an exemption analysis.

The general rule is that when a person files all of their

property becomes part of the bankruptcy estate and is subject to liquidation (sale) by the trustee (the person who administers the case for the benefit of the creditors). Fortunately Congress has recognized that taking everything a person owns to satisfy their debts really isn't much better than a debtor's prison or death. In the extreme case if all assets became property of the bankruptcy estate, then the debtor would have to turn over their clothing to the trustee, the food in the pantry to the trustee, their car, their television, their computer, lawn sprinklers, etc. And I guess in that scenario everyone who filed for bankruptcy would have to show up naked to their creditors meeting to prove that they had given everything over to the trustee. And while that might make the creditors meetings more entertaining to watch, it is unlikely that very many people would go through the process if it was required.

In an effort to be fair and to prevent that type of nonsense, Congress has created a series of exemptions. These exemptions are basically a list of property that you can keep or exempt from becoming part of the bankruptcy estate. Each exemption has a dollar amount limit. The federal exemptions as created by Congress are the most common and worth examining closer. In addition state specific exemptions vary from state to state, which makes them difficult to address in this format. Before filing any type of bankruptcy, you will need to verify which exemptions are available to you and make sure that you appropriately analyze your situation. Many states allow you to choose either the State specific exemptions or the Federal exemptions. In these states you generally are not able to pick and choose between the two, but rather you have to select either Federal or State and then use those exemptions exclusively.

The Federal Bankruptcy Exemptions are found in the Bankruptcy Code at 11 USC § 522 (d). This section of the code lays out in great detail the limits of the various categories of property that are exempt from the bankruptcy estate. One thing to keep in mind though is that they are not automatically exempt; you are required to declare the property you intend to keep by category. In practice this means that if you fail to list something it will become part of the bankruptcy estate and will be subject to sale by the Trustee to satisfy some or all of your debts.

I hesitate to give you specific numbers since they do vary by state and since in many cases these numbers are adjusted on a regular basis for inflation and cost of living changes. The numbers below are accurate as of the time of this writing but may change between now and the publication date of this book and will likely have changed before you read this. In spite of these reservations I have included a complete list of all the federal exemptions in Appendix A at the back of this book.

It is critical that you verify the current exemptions that are in place at the time you are considering a bankruptcy filing and also that you verify which exemptions are available to you. Finally you should make sure that you pick the best available exemptions before you file. If you wait to do so, it may be too late. I have seen many people file for bankruptcy without an attorney or with an attorney who did not advise them properly only to find out that they lost some property that they otherwise could have kept simply by properly analyzing their available exemptions. This is one more example of why I recommend that anyone who is considering bankruptcy consult with a qualified bankruptcy professional, preferably an attorney that spends a significant amount of time working in this area.

For the purposes of illustration, take a brief look at the first five exemptions as laid out in 11 USC § 522 (d) 1-5 below. Keep in mind these may not apply to your situation depending on your jurisdiction or any adjustments that have been made since the time of this writing

1) The debtor's aggregate interest, not to exceed $21,625 in value, in real property or personal property that the debtor or a dependent of the debtor uses as a residence, in a cooperative that owns property that the debtor or a dependent of the debtor uses as a residence, or in a burial plot for the debtor or a dependent of the debtor.

2) The debtor's interest, not to exceed $3,450 in value, in one motor vehicle.

3) The debtor's interest, not to exceed $550 in value in any particular item or $11,525 in aggregate value, in household furnishings, household goods, wearing apparel, appliances, books, animals, crops, or musical instruments, that are held primarily for the personal, family, or household use of the debtor or a dependent of the debtor.

4) The debtor's aggregate interest, not to exceed $1,450 in value, in jewelry held primarily for the personal, family, or household use of the debtor or a dependent of the debtor.

5) The debtor's aggregate interest in any property, not to

exceed in value $1,150 plus up to $10,825 of any unused amount of the exemption provided under paragraph (1) of this subsection.

As you probably noticed the biggest exemption by far is found in§ 522 (d) (1). This exemption, commonly known as the homestead exemption, is limited (as of the time of this writing) to $21,625 in value. OK, so that sounds like a lot but when you think about how much the average home costs, $21,625 dollars really isn't enough.

Married couples get to double this amount if the house is in both their names. Actually they get to double all the exemptions as long as the property is in both names. However if it is in only one of their names then they can only use the exemption to the limit that they have.

Even still, $43,250 (two times the homestead exemption above) really isn't enough to cover most houses. But there is good news. Remember our old friend the security interest? Well as it turns out the value of the security interest is subtracted from the value of the home to determine the value of the debtor's interest in the house. What we are talking about here is how much equity a person has, as opposed to the whole value of the home.

Equity = Total value – Total Debt (value of the security interest)

When you think about this, it makes good sense. After all if a person has house that could sell for $150,000 and owes $125,000 on the house subject to a valid security interest if they sell house they have to pay the first $125,000 to the lender or mortgage holder and then they get to keep the rest after all cost associated with the sale are paid. In this case, the seller would sell the house for $150,000 pay the loan of $125,000, then pay closing costs including a real estate commission and then would get however much is left, probably somewhere around $20,000.

This means that when valuing a piece of property in a bankruptcy it really only makes sense to first deduct the value of any enforceable security interests. A quick note here, sometimes when a lender takes a security interest, they don't follow the procedures required by law, and when this happens, it can dramatically complicate a bankruptcy. If you think that your lender might have made some kind of error, maybe they gave you a title when they should not have or forgot to record a mortgage or whatever make sure that you have a highly trained and respected bankruptcy professional look at the documents before you file for bankruptcy.

In the example above the person had equity of about $25,000. Assume that the same person was married but the house was only in the wife's name because she bought it before they were married. In this case, she would be limited to an exemption of $21,625 and would have equity of $25,000.
If she were to file for bankruptcy she would claim a § 522 (d) (1) exemption of $21,625 and would be leaving $3,375 of her house exposed to possible sale by the trustee. This is what the formula looks like.

$150,000 (value of her house) - $125,000 (value of security interest = $25,000 (her equity)

Then look at her equity

$25,000 (her equity) - $21,625 (her allowable (d) (1) exemption) = $3,375 (her non exempted equity)

Of course, if the trustee were to sell the house she would get to keep the first $21,625 of any money that exceeded the value of the security interest and the closing costs. That may be better than nothing, but remember she didn't want to sell her house at all. She wants to keep her house. So what can she do?

Well one thing she should do is look to see if she has any other exemptions that she can use. In this case, she might be able to use the wild card exemption found in § 522 (d) (5) above. This exemption allows her claim additional equity of $1,150.00. This exemption will be discussed in more detail later, but for now let's see what that does.

> $25,000 (her equity) - $21,625 (her allowable (d) (1) exemption) = $3,375 (her non exempted equity after homestead exemption) - $1,150 (her allowable (d) (5) exemption) = $2,125 (her net non exempt equity).

That's a little better but at this point, she really wishes that her husband was also on the house because then they could use her § 522 (d) (1) exemption of $21,625 and his § 522 (d) (1) exemption of $21,625 giving them plenty of room to exempt all the equity in the house. Unfortunately it is too late to do something about that. If they run out and try to transfer title to the house they will cause a much greater problem. This approach is looked at in the section entitled "What Can Go Wrong and How to Avoid It." For now, trust me, that it would be a very bad idea for her to try and transfer the title to the house in anticipation of a bankruptcy filing.

Now look at a slightly different situation. Instead of buying the house before they were married the couple made the purchase immediately after they were married and it was always in both of their names. The value ($150,000), the loan ($125,000), and of course the equity ($25,000) stayed the same. Clearly, this eliminates the non exempt equity problem demonstrated in the first example.

$150,000 (value of her house) - $125,000 (value of security interest = $25,000 (their equity)

Now look at their equity:

$25,000 (their equity) - $43,250 (their allowable (d) (1) exemption) = <18,250> (their unused portions of the § 522 (d) (1) exemptions)

Technically, it is more accurate to say that they each have $9,125 (one half of $18,250) of unused § 522 (d) (1) exemption. This is important when considering how § 522 (d) (5) is worded.

(5) The debtor's aggregate interest in **any property**, not to exceed in value $1,150 **plus** up to $10,825 of any unused amount of the exemption provided under paragraph (1) of this subsection. (emphasis added)

This wild card exemption can be used for "any property." This means that the debtor can keep cash, gold, silver or whatever as long as they have enough § 522 (d) (5) exemption to cover the value of the property that they list. This is where it gets really good. Notice that § 522 (d) (5) says that the debtor can keep $1,150 PLUS up to $10,825 of their unused § 522 (d) (1) exemption. This means that if a person doesn't use any § 522 (d) (1) exemption then they can keep any property up to $11,975 in value. This is true regardless of how much debt they have and it is in addition to any property otherwise exempted.

Getting back to our married couple above, they can exempt all they equity in their jointly held house ($25,000) and still keep up to $9,125 plus $1150 for a total of $10,275 each in miscellaneous property including cash. So they could have as much as $20,550 in a joint bank account and keep every penny. This is true even if they only owe $15,000 in debt total. This means that theoretically a couple in their situation could file for bankruptcy with more than $20,000 in cash and $25,000 in equity in their house and keep it all. Even if their total debt was less than the money they were holding in cash.

If that couple came in to my office I would tell them to pay off their debts and not file for bankruptcy, but if they choose to do so, they could file and could disclose all of these facts and there would be nothing the trustee or the court or their creditors could do about it.

Understanding exemptions helps you understand why I said that in most cases most filers can keep all of their assets. There are many exemptions, which have not been covered here, for example the retirement account exemption that allows you to keep a nearly unlimited amount in a 401K or an IRA found in § 522 (d) (12). Also not covered is the household good exemption found in § 522 (d) (3), which allows you to keep most or all household goods. Both exemptions are listed in Appendix A.

It is important to keep in mind when looking at exemptions that in some cases the exemptions allowed in the state where you file may be better or worse than the federal exemptions dealt with in this text. Please make sure you verify your exemptions before taking any kind of bankruptcy action.

Case Study #4: Martin and Rebecca

You might recall the school teachers from Case Study #1 where we looked at their fear that other members of their community might find out about their bankruptcy. Their case presents a number of interesting issues when it comes to exemptions. Let's take a quick look back and see what their assets look like in an exemption analysis.

- Their residence is **worth about $200,000** and they owe $225,000. (This is titled in Martin's name only because their lender said they would get a better rate if they did it that way.

- The Lake House (really a small cabin) is **worth about $40,000** (This is titled in Rebecca's name only since it originally belonged to her mother, who sold it to them for one dollar when she moved to Florida ten years ago.

- A 2009 Escalade on which they **owe $22,000** (about what it's worth). It is in both of their names but is driven by Martin.

- A 2007 BMW on which they **owe $3000** (it's **worth about $7000** and it is titled in Rebecca's name alone she bought after selling her first book as a treat to herself).

- Rebecca's Book has sold a few thousand copies but isn't selling at the moment and probably won't unless she makes it big with one of her other books.

- They also have normal amounts of household property plus a very large DVD collection; they generally buy four to five DVDs per week and have been doing so for about 10 years; they estimate that they have over 2,500 DVDs, many of which they have never opened or have only watched one time and have probably spent about $40,000 buying these DVDs.

Let's assume, for now, that there are no qualification issues and that this couple can file for a Chapter 7 bankruptcy and that the only issues facing them are those concerning their exemptions.

> • Residence **worth about $200,000** which they owe $225,000 on. (This is titled in Martin's name only because their lender said they would get a better rate if they did it that way.

Whenever you look at an asset the first question you need to ask is "What is the value of that asset?" This involves thinking about two issues: first, how much money would you get for the property at a sale and second, how much equity is there in the property.

When considering this residence we are given the value of $200,000 so assuming that's true the answer to the first question is $200,000. But you really need to be careful with these values; it is unwise to assume you know the value. If you aren't sure, particularly when there is significant equity, you should get a professional opinion. I recommend hiring a real estate professional to determine a broker's price opinion before filing a bankruptcy. It is very important to establish a good number to use for the equity and can have great consequences if it is done wrong. If the equity is under estimated and the trustee concludes that your value is incorrect any additional equity may be subject to turnover, that is you may be required to give the unexempted equity to the trustee for the benefit of your creditors.

The next thing that you need to look at concerning the residence is the equity figure. Remember the formula is:

Total Value – Total Allowable Secured Interests = Total Equity

$200,000 (value given) - $225,000 (mortgage) = <$25,000> (total equity)

From an exemption perspective any equity number that is less than zero is treated as if it is zero. There is no need to use any exemption in order to keep this residence. If the numbers were different though, for example, if the house was worth $300,000, then the equity would be $75,000 and there would be a problem. Since the property is in Martin's name alone, the rules only allow use of his (d) (1) exemption, which is limited to $21,625. To that we can add his (d) (5) exemption of $1,150 for a total allowable exemption of $22,775. That leaves $52,225 exposed to seizure by the trustee. Fortunately, that was not the issue in this case however it should be noted that if the price estimate of $200,000 was off by $100,000 that it would have caused major issues in the case. This is why it is important to make sure that the values are correct at the time of filing.

> • Lake House (really a small cabin) is worth about $40,000 and titled in Rebecca's name only, since it originally belonged to her mother, who sold it to them for one dollar when she moved to Florida ten years ago.

This house is a bit more problematic. The first problem is that since there is no loan or mortgage against it, the equity is the full value of the property. The formula makes this very clear, since $40,000 minus zero equals $40,000. This equity is attributable to Rebecca alone since the property is titled in her name alone.

Many people's first instinct in this situation would be to apply § 522 (d) (1) just as illustrated in the previous example above. However a careful reading of the wording of the (d) (1) exemption illustrates a fundamental flaw with this reaction.

(1) The debtor's aggregate interest, not to exceed $21,625 in value, in <u>real property</u> or personal property that the debtor or a dependent of the debtor <u>uses as a residence</u>, in a cooperative that owns property that the debtor or a dependent of the debtor uses as a residence, or in a burial plot for the debtor or a dependent of the debtor.

I have underlined the critical issues. First the residence must be real property (commonly known as real estate) and second it must be used by debtor or a dependent of the debtor as a residence. In this case, the lake house (cabin) is clearly real property, however it is not used as a residence by Rebecca or any of her dependants. This means that she cannot use this exemption and that if she attempts to, the exemption will be disallowed by the court potentially causing her to lose the right to exempt any portion of the property. This would be a very expensive mistake.

So this leaves the (d) (5) or wild card exemption, which says that the debtor can exempt property (of any kind) up to $1,150 plus up to $10,825 of the unused portion of the debtor's (d) (1) exemption. Since she has no personal residence in her name and hasn't otherwise used any of her (d) (1) exemption she is entitled to exempt $11,975 in equity in this property. This leave a significant portion ($28,025) of the equity in this property exposed to potential sale by the trustee.

• 2009 Escalade on which they owe $22,000 (about what it's worth). The vehicle is in both of their names, but is driven by Martin.

By now you likely recognize that this asset or property does not present an exemption issue because there is no equity.

If there was equity then we would have to look at the exemptions and see which one fit this type of property. You may want to look in Appendix A at the exemptions and see if you can figure out which exemption would be used to cover this type of property if there was equity to exempt. (Hint this is a motor vehicle).

> • 2007 BMW on which they owe $3,000 (it's worth about $7,000). It is titled in Rebecca's name alone she bought after selling her first book as a treat to herself.

OK, if you didn't figure out that last one, I am about to give you the answer, because this is the same situation. The first thing to do when analyzing an exemption is to find the value. In this case we were given it. The next thing is to calculate the equity. Assuming that the value is correct and the amount still owed is correct, this vehicle has about $4,000 dollars in equity. A quick reminder that this number is calculated by taking the value of $7,000 and subtracting the secured interest of $3,000.

After finding the value of the debtor's interest, we then look at the exemptions and attempt to fully exempt that value. The clearest exemption here is found in 11 USC § 522 (d) (2) also known as the motor vehicle exemption.

> • The debtor's interest, not to exceed $3,450 in value, in one motor vehicle.

So the good news is that the first $3,450 is exempt, the bad news is that we used up Rebecca's (d) (5) Wildcard above so the other $550 is not exempt. This is where valuation becomes critical. How do we know that the value is $4,000? A dealer's opinion or an online price guide can be very helpful in this situation, but assuming the value is correct then we are left with only two options. One, we can leave a portion non exempt or two, we can amend our exemption on the lake house to leave a greater portion non exempt. This second choice is available to us because we used the wildcard to exempt that property.

> • Rebecca's Book (it has sold a few thousand copies but isn't selling at the moment and probably won't unless she makes it big with one of her other books)

This presents an interesting issue from a bankruptcy perspective. What is the value of the copyright to a book that isn't selling? The answer is not very clear at all, and a lot of it depends on the trustee. Some trustees that I have dealt with would say its minimal value and really wouldn't argue with any reasonable value. On the other hand, they would be well within their rights to request a professional evaluation of the value. And if this valuation exceeded the value listed by Rebecca then she would risk losing the rights to her book.

The second issue with this book is that the only exemption that applies is the wildcard or (d) (5) exemption and we have already used this one up.

> • The couple also has normal amounts of household property plus a very large DVD collection. They generally buy four to five DVDs per week and have been doing so for about 10 years; they estimate that they have over 2,500 DVDs, many of which they have never opened or have only watched one time. They have probably spent about $40,000 buying these DVDs.

The final piece of property to deal with is this unusually large DVD collection. Determining the value of this collection is quite interesting. When they first came in to talk to me, they told me that this collection was worth at least $25,000. When looking at any valuation question it is important to remember that in bankruptcy we are dealing with liquidation values. Ultimately the trustee will only fight about values when they think they can get more than the value scheduled by the debtor on the bankruptcy forms. At the end of the day, the trustee's job is to take as much as possible from the debtor and give to the creditors. However, if they take over a DVD collection they then have to sell it. Remember a Chapter 7 is a liquidation bankruptcy. This means that the trustee needs to sell it quickly. If tasked with selling a collection of DVDs, most trustees I know would offer them for sale as a lot and probably for less than a buck a piece. Given this, a safe number of the value of these DVDs is probably around $2,500 not $25,000.

As far as exemptions go, these can likely slide through under household goods the (d) (3) exemption, which has plenty of room. Our school teacher friends have other household goods as well be this exemption is very generous and likely will not be an issue.

So where are we at with Martin and Rebecca? Below I have listed their currently scheduled assets and exemptions in a manner similar to what you would see on their bankruptcy schedules. Note all property is also listed on either schedule A (real property) or schedule B (personal property) depending.

Schedule C

Property	Exemption law	Value of Exemption	Current Value w/o deducting Exemption
Lake House	D(5)	$11,975.00	$40,000.00
2007 BMW	D(3)	$3,450.00	$4,000.00
DVDs	D(2)	$2,500.00	$2,500.00

Note there likely would be additional entries for household goods, bank accounts etc but these have been eliminated for simplicity. The key issue is to make sure that every item claimed to be exempt is listed on this form.

In summary, whenever you are looking at exemption issues, you need to go through the following process:

• Think about value. How much is the property really worth? (By property we mean any item of value whether real estate, stocks, cash, clothing or whatever, in other words pretty much anything) What can it be sold for? This is a liquidation analysis so often we are talking about garage sale prices, a new suit might cost $500 dollars, but its resale value might only be $15 or $20, a used DVD might only be $1 or $2.

• How much equity does the property have? Run the formula:

Total Value – Total Allowable Secured Interests = Total Equity

• Look at all available Exemptions. Don't forget the Wild Card

• If you don't have room to exempt it look at your other options (i.e. a Chapter 13 or a short term payment plan with Chapter 7 trustee). Just because you can't exempt something doesn't necessarily mean that you will lose it.

• Be creative: this is where a good attorney who has a relationship with the trustees in question is extra helpful. There probably is a way to work it out with the trustee. The secret is to negotiate a fair agreement or settlement with the trustee. Your attorney will need to be proactive in this manner and should be well versed in bankruptcy before undertaking this type of transaction.

TYPES OF BANKRUPTCY/CHOOSING THE RIGHT ONE FOR YOU

There are several types of bankruptcy relief available to debtors, including certain specialty types such as the Chapter 9 bankruptcy, which provides for reorganization of cities and other municipalities, and the Chapter 11 bankruptcy, which deals with the reorganization of businesses. These types are beyond the scope of this writing. For a complete list of types of bankruptcies see the glossary at the back of this book.

This section will discuss the two most common consumer bankruptcies the Chapter 7 and Chapter 13 bankruptcies. We will do this by looking once again at Martin and Rebecca, for as you may recall, we left a number of unresolved exemption issues in their case.

If they were to file a Chapter 7 bankruptcy with the exemptions listed, the Chapter 7 Trustee would be able to seize and sell their BMW and also their Lake House. Obviously, this was not Rebecca and Martin's desired result.

In the beginning of this book, we learned that a Chapter 13 bankruptcy differs from a Chapter 7 in one fundamental way, and that is, that in a Chapter 13 the debtor repays all or some of the debts owed to their creditors. This is true whether or not those debts were or would have been otherwise dischargeable. It is clear from this distinction that for many people a Chapter 7 is financially beneficial as repaying none of their debts is far better than repaying all or even a portion of their debts.

Upon explaining this distinction I am often asked why any person would choose to file for a Chapter 13 bankruptcy.

The answer to this question is actually quite simple. There are two primary reasons why a person would choose a Chapter 13 over a Chapter 7. The most obvious would be if they did not qualify for a Chapter 7, once a Chapter 7 is no longer an option the prospect of discharging a portion of their debts and while getting the instant relief of the automatic stay suddenly sounds very attractive. The second reason a person might choose to file a Chapter 13 over a Chapter 7 even when they qualify for a Chapter 7 is if there is some piece of property or asset which they wouldn't be able to keep in a Chapter 7 that they could keep in a Chapter 13.

Essentially all people who seek debt relief qualify for some form of bankruptcy. But you may be wondering, what it takes to qualify for the most coveted form the Chapter 7. The code is fairly clear on what it takes to qualify.

To qualify for relief under Chapter 7 of the Bankruptcy Code, the debtor may be an individual, a partnership, or a corporation or other business entity. Further Chapter 7 relief is available irrespective of the amount of the debtor's debts or whether the debtor is solvent or insolvent. There are however some limitations to Chapter 7 relief. For example, an individual cannot file under Chapter 7 or any other chapter if during the preceding 180 days a prior bankruptcy petition was dismissed due to the debtor's willful failure to appear before the court or comply with orders of the court, or the debtor voluntarily dismissed the previous case after creditors sought relief from the bankruptcy court to recover property upon which they hold liens. In addition, no individual may be a debtor under Chapter 7 or any chapter of the Bankruptcy Code unless he or she has, within 180 days before filing, received credit counseling from an approved credit counseling agency either in an individual or group briefing.

The final and most important qualification issue is found in 11 U.S.C. § 707 (b) (1) where code requires that all debtor's whose income exceeds their State's median income be subjected to a means test to determine whether the filing of the Chapter 7 is presumptively abusive.

Abuse is presumed if the debtor's aggregate current monthly income over 5 years, net of certain statutorily allowed expenses, is more than (i) $11,725, or (ii) 25% of the debtor's nonpriority unsecured debt, as long as that amount is at least $7,025. (2) The debtor may rebut a presumption of abuse only by a showing of special circumstances that justify additional expenses or adjustments of current monthly income. Unless the debtor overcomes the presumption of abuse, the case will generally be converted to Chapter 13 (with the debtor's consent) or will be dismissed.

Essentially what this means is that certain higher income individuals may not qualify for protection under Chapter 7 of the Bankruptcy Code. While some debtors have found this to be a burden the underlying policy, consideration seems to be that if an individual has the ability to pay some of their debts then perhaps they should pay some of their debts. When you consider this policy it makes reasonable sense. For example, if an individual makes a quarter million dollars a year, should they really walk completely free of their debts? Is this fair to their creditors or to society in general? But what if the person owes five million or more? Do we want to put them in a position where they have no possible relief and their income is seized forever with no reasonable chance to ever pay off their debts? It is for this very type of situation that a Chapter 13 bankruptcy was designed.

The previous example is an extreme case but it does illustrate the underlying principle involved in the creation of the means test. The entire form title B22a can be found at the back of this book in Appendix C.   While this form appears complicated, it actually is fairly self explanatory. The form starts with a declaration of income, continues with allowable expenses, and finishes with a projection of current disposable income. Instructions for the completion of this form is beyond the scope of this book.

The critical thing to remember is that if a debtor's income is below their State's median or average income for their family size then no presumption of abuse arises and they automatically will qualify under the means test. I have included a table of the current median incomes by state at the back of this book in Appendix D. One other thing to keep in mind is that the means test is not required for debtors whose debts are primarily non consumer debts. This means that if your debts are more than 50 percent business debts you are not required to complete the means test.

The main reason a person would choose to file a Chapter 13 bankruptcy when they qualify for a Chapter 7 is that filing a Chapter 7 will result in them losing some property that they would prefer to keep. There are essentially two situations where this would occur: the first is in the case of non exempt property such as we have seen in Martin and Rebecca's case, the second and far more common situation occurs when a person is behind on a secured piece of property and wishes to keep that property. In a Chapter 7, an individual needs to be current on secured property, such as their mortgage or their car note if they want to keep the property. In a Chapter 13 bankruptcy, a person can stop the pending action as so long as they haven't already lost that property to foreclosure or seizure. It is possible to preserve their interest in the property by way of the automatic stay provided that they create a plan to repay the debt and to make the debt current before the end of the plans duration.

When determining whether to file a Chapter 7 or a Chapter 13, you must always consider first whether you qualify for a 7, and secondly, if you qualify, you need to take a close look at your property. Ask yourself are you current on you mortgages and car loans etc? Take a look at your property, go through an exemption analysis to determine if you can you keep all your property. If not is that a problem? Do you want to commit yourself to three to five years worth of payments simply to keep the non exempted property? It is essential that you think these issues through carefully before filing any bankruptcy. If you are unsure, make sure you get good advice from a competent professional.

Take a quick look back at Martin and Rebecca. As you will recall, they have a couple of issues that might make a Chapter 13 more appealing to them. The most obvious of these issues is the large amount of non exempt property that they have and would like to keep. However, they have a more pressing issue than that, they both have jobs at a public school and their children are grown and out of the house. Their income at the time they came to see me was approximately $100,000 a year. For a family of two, this income greatly exceeds the median income in their state. This doesn't mean that they do not qualify but rather that they need to complete the means test.

The means test allows for deductions for clothing, insurance, secured debt payments among many other allowable deductions. As I indicated previously, the intricacies of the means test are beyond this writing, however you might find it interesting that Martin and Rebecca's various expenses where such that they just barely qualified for a Chapter 7.

In spite of the fact that they did technically qualify for a Chapter 7, they elected to file for a chapter 13 in order to keep the property they were unable to exempt. As you probably remember, they were unable to exempt a significant portion of their lake house and they were unable to exempt a small portion of Rebecca's BMW. It would appear that they were left with essentially two options they could allow for the liquidation of the lake house, or apply part of the proceeds to exempt the reminder of the car. Or they could File a Chapter 13 and pay in enough over the course of their plan to cover the unexempted amount.

A creative bankruptcy practitioner would likely see a number of other possible options, including mortgaging the lake house and turning over the money proceeds of the loan to a Chapter 7 trustee as non exempt money. Another option that I considered with them was the possibility of moving to the lake house and giving up the current personal residence, thereby being able to exempt the higher homestead amount as opposed to being limited to the (d)(5) wild card exemption. These types of creative options should be used with great caution and should only be considered when one has a complete understanding of the relevant law. There are numerous pitfalls to be avoided and one must be very careful ensure that whatever actions they take are not in violation of the law.

In spite of these options they elected to file for a Chapter 13. Under the terms of their plan they were required to pay all of their disposable income for a 36 month period and further had to pay a minimum amount equal to their unexempted property. This second requirement is the product of what is commonly called a liquidation analysis which requires that a debtor pay at least as much to creditors as they would have in a Chapter 7.

As you can see there are a number of issues to consider when filing Chapter 13 bankruptcy. In this book, we have only covered a small portion of the total issues to consider. The careful creation of a repayment plan is essential to the successful completion of a Chapter 13. At the completion of the plan any remaining dischargeable debts receive a discharge and the case is closed.

HOW A CASE WORKS
AND WHAT TO EXPECT

At this point you should have a fairly good understanding of the major issues that need to be considered when thinking about filing for bankruptcy. You should be able to identify issues that may require additional reading or investigation. The one area we haven't covered is how one goes about filing a case and what happens once it is filed.

The process can be anything but straight forward. All cases require a petition for bankruptcy and several related schedules. One schedule was previously examined in the discussion about exemptions. I have included a complete set of schedules, the voluntary petition, the means test, and statement of financial affairs in the various appendixes to this book. Each of these documents is required and the typical initial filing for bankruptcy runs 40 pages or more. The requirement to file these documents should not be taken lightly; I have seen numerous cases filed by individuals and by some less experienced attorneys dismissed from court for failure to file required documents.

Another strict requirement is the provision of the code that requires pre filing and post filing credit counseling. Failure to receive the pre filing credit counseling prior to filing for bankruptcy mandates the denial of discharge. The courts are given no discretion in this area of the statute and will dismiss your case without discharge. If this happens you will not receive the benefit of the bankruptcy filed. For this reason it is very important that you complete an approved pre filing credit counseling course no more than 180 days before the day of your filing.

You are also required to file a second certificate proving that you took a budgeting course after filing. Neither of these courses need to be difficult and should take less than an hour or two each. Your local court should be able to provide you with a list of the approved agencies for your area. Most bankruptcy attorneys and even most document prep companies can help with locating an approved provider. This counseling is often done over the phone or on the web and shouldn't cost more than $30 or $40 dollars. One last thing to remember is that this counseling must have been done within 180 days of your filing date so don't do it now and then wait eight or nine months to file or you will be denied discharge.

The following is a list of the major documents required for a chapter seven filing.

- Statement of Social Security Number
- Statement of Current Monthly Income and Means Test Calculation
- Debtor's Certification of Completion of Instructional Course Concerning Financial Management
- Voluntary petition
- Cover Sheet for Schedules
- Summary of Schedules (Includes Statistical Summary of Certain Liabilities)
- Schedule A – Real Property
- Schedule B – Personal Property
- Schedule C – Property Claimed as Exempt
- Schedule D – Creditors Holding Secured Claims
- Schedule E – Creditors Holding Unsecure Priority Claims
- Schedule F – Creditors Holding Unsecured Nonpriority Claims
- Schedule G – Executory Contracts and Unexpired Leases
- Schedule H – Codebtors
- Schedule I – Current Income of Individual Debtor
- Schedule J – Current Expenditures of Individual

Debtor
• Declaration Concerning Debtor's Schedules
• Statement of Financial Affairs
• Individual Debtor's Statement of Intention

Additionally a Chapter 13 filing will require the filing of a Chapter 13 Plan which includes a method of payment, a payment percentage to unsecured creditors, and a plan arrangement.

Since this is not a do it yourself book, detail about how to fill out these forms is not included, but there are many resources available that can help you with this process. Again I caution that it is very important to get these things done correctly and accurately. If you have any doubts about this process, you should contact a qualified and experienced bankruptcy professional.

After preparing all of these documents you are ready to file your case. It is at the point of filing that the automatic stay takes effect. Cases are typically filed electronically with the court. When you file it will necessary at to pay the appropriate filing fee which varies depending on the type of case you are filing but should be around $300.

Shortly after filing you will receive a notice from the court appointing a trustee and establishing a date for a section 341 meeting also known as a meeting of the creditors. At this meeting, the trustee (and potentially your creditors) will have an opportunity to question you, the debtor, about the truth and accuracy of your filings. This meeting typically is short and sweet. If all the documents were prepared correctly and if your case is otherwise routine, this meeting should last no longer than ten minutes.

Typically the trustee will ask the debtor under oath if

they read and understood their filings and if all the information contained therein is truthful and accurate. After verifying the schedules, the trustee will ask any necessary follow up questions and conclude the meeting. It is rare for any actual creditors to show up at the meeting since it is the trustee's job to represent the creditors throughout the course of the bankruptcy.

For many, if not most debtors, this is the only time that they ever see their trustee and they never have occasion to see their assigned Judge. It is important to understand that the role of the trustee is to collect as much money as possible. In a Chapter 7, in most cases the trustee collects nothing. For this reason, these meetings are short and are geared toward identifying those limited cases where there are non-exempt assets. By focusing their efforts on those cases, the trustees maximize their own returns as well, since they generally receive a small percentage of the recovery.

In a Chapter 13 bankruptcy the trustee has an incentive to spend more time with each individual debtor because they receive fees from most Chapter 13 cases.

Sometime after filing and before your discharge, you will have to complete a second credit counseling course that will provide you with information regarding budgeting and credit. Proof that this course has been completed will need to be filed with the court. You will also need to make sure that any reaffirmation agreements that you are entering into are signed and filed with the court for approval.

Other than that you wait. In about three or four months you should receive a notice of discharge directly from the court, and a while after that your case will close and then you are pretty much done. There are a couple of issues that could come up, but with the exception of inheriting money or winning the lottery, there isn't much that can go wrong if you were honest and complete in your filings and testimony.

WHAT CAN GO WRONG AND HOW TO AVOID IT?

This is a tricky topic to write about because there are numerous things that can go wrong, and I think it would be irresponsible to try to list them all here. Any attempt to do so would certainly miss many possible problems. The critical issue for all debtors is to be forthcoming and honest. It is a major violation of federal law to attempt to hide any assets while in bankruptcy. Hiding assets or income can very well land the debtor in prison.

The biggest risk to an honest debtor is failure to properly disclose or exempt property. Failure to properly exempt can result in a loss of the property in question. For this reason I strongly recommend that you get good quality legal advice before even considering filing for bankruptcy.

So how do you avoid problems? Be honest and make sure you understand what it is you are doing and why. A bankruptcy doesn't have to be the end of your financial health, in fact when used properly and done correctly a bankruptcy can be the fresh start it is designed to be. Use this book to give you an idea of the information that you need to know and to educate yourself, so that when you move forward (if you move forward) you will be better prepared, and you will be able to search out and find competent a bankruptcy attorney. After having read this book you should be able to quickly determine if the attorney you are considering has the requisite knowledge to properly represent you. They should be able to answer your questions on the issues covered in this book and more.

Keep in mind that this book is not intended to give you the information necessary to file your own bankruptcy but rather is intended to give you an overview of the topics involved so that when you can make the right choice about whether or not to move forward. Your next step should be to seek out a competent bankruptcy attorney. This is usually someone who files 50 or more cases a year, but the total number of filings alone isn't enough. They should also be able answer your questions clearly but more importantly they should ask you the right questions. At the minimum they should ask you about your income, expenses, assets, and debts.

The most important thing you can do for yourself if you decide to move forward with a filing is find a competent attorney and give them all the information that they need to fully understand your position. Avoid mass filing bankruptcy groups or organizations where you never meet your attorney, make sure you get some face time with the attorney you hire. Don't use document preparation services and assume that since you read this book you don't need an attorney. This book is not a substitute for competent legal advice.

A large percentage of the problems that I have seen in come up in bankruptcy were avoidable. They typically were the result of a person either attempting to do it on their own or the result of an attorney thinking they would give bankruptcy a try. If your attorney hasn't been involved in this area of the law recently then you should use extreme caution.

On the other hand, if you hire a good attorney and invest the time necessary to ensure they fully understands your complete financial situation, the process should go smoothly and you soon have the fresh start that bankruptcy promises.

OK, I FILED WHAT DO I DO NOW?

At this point you can stop and take a deep breath. You have finished the hard part, and if all went well, you have your discharge in hand and a fresh start in front of you. Most former debtors report that this moment is quite freeing. The relief of pressure experienced upon filing is intensified when the discharge is received.

The good news is that your credit will take care of itself. If you pay your bills on time and don't over load yourself with new debts, your credit will heal itself. The amount of time it takes to repair your credit is dependent on you. It takes 10 years for the Chapter 7 bankruptcy to clear off your credit report for good. So the worse case you wait 10 years, but the good news is that you can repair credit much faster by taking a few simple steps.

• Pay whatever bills you have on time all the time. You no longer have any margin for error. I don't think that this should be too difficult since you no longer are overwhelmed by debt.
• Get a small credit card or a store card. Use it a little but make sure you pay it off every month

Perhaps buy a single tank of gas a month on it. Whatever you do make sure you put the cash away to pay it off you can't afford to fall back into the same situation. This will take discipline but it is worth the effort.

Establishing good credit takes work but it is fundamentally about having a low debt burden relative to your income and paying your bills on time. Once the bankruptcy is complete you should have already reduced your debt burden. All that is left is to pay your bills on time.

You are better off not having credit than abusing credit. It's up to you, but if you aren't sure that you can handle a credit card then don't get one. Don't go finance a car at 18 percent interest. Make smart decisions and you will be able to buy a car for cash or at the very least get a reasonable interest rate. If you are considering a big purchase, put the projected payment amount away for a couple of months before hand. This will do two very important things for you. One it will show you if you can afford the payment. If you are having trouble saving the amount of the payment then it is probably too high. You should also save and put away the amount of an increase in costs associated with the purchase (extra insurance, fuel, etc.) The second reason to do this is it creates a buffer for you if something changes. If you keep two months expenses on this purchase in a separate account the money will be there if an emergency occurs.

Finally before you buy anything or get any credit, do yourself a favor. Make sure you understand how much you make and where it goes. Write a budget, they may not be fun but a good budget is almost guaranteed to improve your credit and your life over the long run. You will be able to see what you can and cannot afford. You will be able accurately understand your true financial picture. This kind of understanding is essential to avoid the mistakes that got you to where you were.

You're done now, you can't change the past but you can make sure it doesn't happen again. I wish you the best of luck and know that you can get through this process. I have helped hundreds through it and my colleagues have helped millions. There is no reason that a bankruptcy should ruin your life.

A Final Note

Reading this book does not qualify you as an expert in bankruptcy law or its consequences. This book is only intended to give you a general overview of some of the issues that need to be considered in the bankruptcy context. Please do not move forward with a bankruptcy without getting independent legal advice.

Since every situation is unique, it is imperative that you have your situation reviewed by a person in your area qualified to give you legal advice. Do not assume this book is necessarily correct. I have made every effort to be accurate but the law varies from jurisdiction to jurisdiction and from time to time. The law is always in flux and always can change. Therefore you cannot rely on this book, or any other, as your sole reference. You must get up to date and jurisdiction specific advice before deciding whether to proceed with any form of debt relief.

I wish you the best as you consider this process. Under the right circumstances bankruptcy can be a good option and can provide great relief but it is not to be taken lightly. This book is not intended to form an attorney client relationship between us and is not an attempt to solicit your business. For this reason, I ask that you do not try to contact me for advice based upon information that you learned. Thank you for taking the time to read this book. I hope that you found it helpful,

Jeffrey D. Holst

APPENDIX A: FEDERAL EXEMPTIONS

Exemptions change over time and it is important to select the correct exemption statute as provided by your individual state or jurisdiction. Many states allow the Federal Exemptions as outlined in 11 USC § 522 (d) and it is for this reason that I have included these here. You should use these only as reference and should verify which exemptions are allowed by your jurisdiction before filing any type of bankruptcy action. For information on how these exemptions work please refer back to the section entitled "What Can I Keep?"

1) The debtor's aggregate interest, not to exceed $21,625 in value, in real property or personal property that the debtor or a dependent of the debtor uses as a residence, in a cooperative that owns property that the debtor or a dependent of the debtor uses as a residence, or in a burial plot for the debtor or a dependent of the debtor.

2) The debtor's interest, not to exceed $3,450 in value, in one motor vehicle.

3) The debtor's interest, not to exceed $550 in value in any particular item or $11,525 in aggregate value, in household furnishings, household goods, wearing apparel, appliances, books, animals, crops, or musical instruments, that are held primarily for the personal, family, or household use of the debtor or a dependent of the debtor.

4) The debtor's aggregate interest, not to exceed $1,450 in value, in jewelry held primarily for the personal, family, or household use of the debtor or a dependent of the debtor.

5) The debtor's aggregate interest in any property, not to exceed in value $1,150 plus up to $10,825 of any unused amount of the exemption provided under para-

graph (1) of this subsection.

6)   The debtor's aggregate interest, not to exceed $2,175 in value, in any implements, professional books, or tools, of the trade of the debtor or the trade of a dependent of the debtor.

7)   Any unmatured life insurance contract owned by the debtor, other than a credit life insurance contract.

8)   The debtor's aggregate interest, not to exceed in value $11,525 less any amount of property of the estate transferred in the manner specified in section 542(d) of this title, in any accrued dividend or interest under, or loan value of, any unmatured life insurance contract owned by the debtor under which the insured is the debtor or an individual of whom the debtor is a dependent.

9)   Professionally prescribed health aids for the debtor or a dependent of the debtor.

10)   The debtor's right to receive–

A- a social security benefit, unemployment compensation, or a local public assistance benefit;

B- a veterans' benefit;

C- a disability, illness, or unemployment benefit;

D- alimony, support, or separate maintenance, to the extent reasonably necessary for the support of the debtor and any dependent of the debtor;

E- a payment under a stock bonus, pension, profit sharing, annuity, or similar plan or contract on account of illness, disability, death, age, or length of service, to the extent reasonably necessary for the support of the debtor and any dependent of the debtor, unless–

F- such plan or contract was established by or under the auspices of an insider that employed the debtor at the time the debtor's rights under such plan or contract arose;

G- such payment is on account of age or length of service; and

H- such plan or contract does not qualify under section 401(a), 403(a), 403(b), or 408 of the Internal Revenue Code of 1986.

I- The debtor's right to receive, or property that is traceable to–

J- an award under a crime victim's reparation law;

K- a payment on account of the wrongful death of an individual of whom the debtor was a dependent, to the extent reasonably necessary for the support of the debtor and any dependent of the debtor;

L- a payment under a life insurance contract that insured the life of an individual of whom the debtor was a dependent on the date of such individual's death, to the extent reasonably necessary for the support of the debtor and any dependent of the debtor;

M- a payment, not to exceed $21,625, on account of personal bodily injury, not including pain and suffering or compensation for actual pecuniary loss, of the debtor or an individual of whom the debtor is a dependent; or

N- a payment in compensation of loss of future earnings of the debtor or an individual of whom the debtor is or was a dependent, to the extent reasonably necessary for the support of the debtor and any dependent of the debtor.

12)   Retirement funds to the extent that those funds are in a fund or account that is exempt from taxation under section 401, 403, 408, 408A, 414, 457, or 501(a) of the Internal Revenue Code of 1986.

APPENDIX B:
11 USC § 362 AUTOMATIC STAY

(a) Except as provided in subsection (b) of this section, a petition filed under section 301, 302, or 303 of this title, or an application filed under section 5(a)(3) of the Securities Investor Protection Act of 1970, operates as a stay, applicable to all entities, of--

(1) the commencement or continuation, including the issuance or employment of process, of a judicial, administrative, or other action or proceeding against the debtor that was or could have been commenced before the commencement of the case under this title, or to recover a claim against the debtor that arose before the commencement of the case under this title;

(2) the enforcement, against the debtor or against property of the estate, of a judgment obtained before the commencement of the case under this title;

(3) any act to obtain possession of property of the estate or of property from the estate or to exercise control over property of the estate;

(4) any act to create, perfect, or enforce any lien against property of the estate;

(5) any act to create, perfect, or enforce against property

of the debtor any lien to the extent that such lien secures a claim that arose before the commencement of the case under this title;

(6) any act to collect, assess, or recover a claim against the debtor that arose before the commencement of the case under this title;

(7) the setoff of any debt owing to the debtor that arose before the commencement of the case under this title against any claim against the debtor; and

(8) the commencement or continuation of a proceeding before the United States Tax Court concerning a corporate debtor's tax liability for a taxable period the bankruptcy court may determine or concerning the tax liability of a debtor who is an individual for a taxable period ending before the date of the order for relief under this title.

(b) The filing of a petition under section 301, 302, or 303 of this title, or of an application under section 5(a)(3) of the Securities Investor Protection Act of 1970, does not operate as a stay--

(1) under subsection (a) of this section, of the commencement or continuation of a criminal action or proceeding against the debtor;

(2) under subsection (a)--
    (A) of the commencement or continuation of a civil

action or proceeding--

(i) for the establishment of paternity;

(ii) for the establishment or modification of an order for domestic support obligations;

(iii) concerning child custody or visitation;

(iv) for the dissolution of a marriage, except to the extent that such proceeding seeks to determine the division of property that is property of the estate; or

(v) regarding domestic violence;

(B) of the collection of a domestic support obligation from property that is not property of the estate;

(C) with respect to the withholding of income that is property of the estate or property of the debtor for payment of a domestic support obligation under a judicial or administrative order or a statute;

(D) of the withholding, suspension, or restriction of a driver's license, a professional or occupational license, or a recreational license, under State law, as specified in section 466(a)(16) of the Social Security Act;

(E) of the reporting of overdue support owed by a parent to any consumer reporting agency as specified in section 466(a)(7) of the Social Security Act;

(F) of the interception of a tax refund, as specified in sections 464 and 466(a)(3) of the Social Security Act or under an analogous State law; or

(G) of the enforcement of a medical obligation, as specified under title IV of the Social Security Act;

(3) under subsection (a) of this section, of any act to per-

fect, or to maintain or continue the perfection of, an interest in property to the extent that the trustee's rights and powers are subject to such perfection under section 546(b) of this title or to the extent that such act is accomplished within the period provided under section 547(e) (2)(A) of this title;

(4) under paragraph (1), (2), (3), or (6) of subsection (a) of this section, of the commencement or continuation of an action or proceeding by a governmental unit or any organization exercising authority under the Convention on the Prohibition of the Development, Production, Stockpiling and Use of Chemical Weapons and on Their Destruction, opened for signature on January 13, 1993, to enforce such governmental unit's or organization's police and regulatory power, including the enforcement of a judgment other than a money judgment, obtained in an action or proceeding by the governmental unit to enforce such governmental unit's or organization's police or regulatory power;

(5) Repealed. Pub. L. 105–277, div. I, title VI, § 603(1), Oct. 21, 1998, 112 Stat. 2681–866;]

(6) under subsection (a) of this section, of the setoff by a commodity broker, forward contract merchant, stockbroker, financial institution, financial participant, or securities clearing agency of any mutual debt and claim under or in connection with commodity contracts, as defined in section 761 of this title, forward contracts, or securi-

ties contracts, as defined in section 741 of this title, that constitutes the setoff of a claim against the debtor for a margin payment, as defined in section 101, 741, or 761 of this title, or settlement payment, as defined in section 101 or 741 of this title, arising out of commodity contracts, forward contracts, or securities contracts against cash, securities, or other property held by, pledged to, under the control of, or due from such commodity broker, forward contract merchant, stockbroker, financial institution, financial participant, or securities clearing agency to margin, guarantee, secure, or settle commodity contracts, forward contracts, or securities contracts;

(7) under subsection (a) of this section, of the setoff by a repo participant or financial participant, of any mutual debt and claim under or in connection with repurchase agreements that constitutes the setoff of a claim against the debtor for a margin payment, as defined in section 741, or 761 of this title, or settlement payment, as defined in section 741 of this title, arising out of repurchase agreements against cash, securities, or other property held by, pledged to, under the control of, or due from such repo participant or financial participant to margin, guarantee, secure or settle repurchase agreements;

(8) under subsection (a) of this section, of the commencement of any action by the Secretary of Housing and Urban Development to foreclose a mortgage or deed of trust in any case in which the mortgage or deed of trust held by the Secretary is insured or was formerly insured under

the National Housing Act and covers property, or com-
binations of property, consisting of five or more living
units;

(9) under subsection (a), of--
(A) an audit by a governmental unit to determine tax liability;
(B) the issuance to the debtor by a governmental unit of a notice
of tax deficiency;
(C) a demand for tax returns; or
(D) the making of an assessment for any tax and issuance of a
notice and demand for payment of such an assessment (but any
tax lien that would otherwise attach to property of the estate by
reason of such an assessment shall not take effect unless such
tax is a debt of the debtor that will not be discharged in the case
and such property or its proceeds are transferred out of the estate to, or otherwise revested in, the debtor).

(10) under subsection (a) of this section, of any act by a lessor
to the debtor under a lease of nonresidential real property that
has terminated by the expiration of the stated term of the lease
before the commencement of or during a case under this title to
obtain possession of such property;

(11) under subsection (a) of this section, of the presentment of a
negotiable instrument and the giving of notice of and protesting
dishonor of such an instrument;

(12) under subsection (a) of this section, after the date which is
90 days after the filing of such petition, of the commencement
or continuation, and conclusion to the entry of final judgment,

of an action which involves a debtor subject to reorganization pursuant to chapter 11 of this title and which was brought by the Secretary of Transportation under section 31325 of title 46 (including distribution of any proceeds of sale) to foreclose a preferred ship or fleet mortgage, or a security interest in or relating to a vessel or vessel under construction, held by the Secretary of Transportation under section 207 or title XI of the Merchant Marine Act, 1936, or under applicable State law;

(13) under subsection (a) of this section, after the date which is 90 days after the filing of such petition, of the commencement or continuation, and conclusion to the entry of final judgment, of an action which involves a debtor subject to reorganization pursuant to chapter 11 of this title and which was brought by the Secretary of Commerce under section 31325 of title 46 (including distribution of any proceeds of sale) to foreclose a preferred ship or fleet mortgage in a vessel or a mortgage, deed of trust, or other security interest in a fishing facility held by the Secretary of Commerce under section 207 or title XI of the Merchant Marine Act, 1936;

(14) under subsection (a) of this section, of any action by an accrediting agency regarding the accreditation status of the debtor as an educational institution;

(15) under subsection (a) of this section, of any action by a State licensing body regarding the licensure of the debtor as an educational institution;

(16) under subsection (a) of this section, of any action by a guar-

anty agency, as defined in section 435(j) of the Higher Education Act of 1965 or the Secretary of Education regarding the eligibility of the debtor to participate in programs authorized under such Act;

(17) under subsection (a), of the setoff by a swap participant or financial participant of a mutual debt and claim under or in connection with one or more swap agreements that constitutes the setoff of a claim against the debtor for any payment or other transfer of property due from the debtor under or in connection with any swap agreement against any payment due to the debtor from the swap participant or financial participant under or in connection with any swap agreement or against cash, securities, or other property held by, pledged to, under the control of, or due from such swap participant or financial participant to margin, guarantee, secure, or settle any swap agreement;

(18) under subsection (a) of the creation or perfection of a statutory lien for an ad valorem property tax, or a special tax or special assessment on real property whether or not ad valorem, imposed by a governmental unit, if such tax or assessment comes due after the date of the filing of the petition;

(19) under subsection (a), of withholding of income from a debtor's wages and collection of amounts withheld, under the debtor's agreement authorizing that withholding and collection for the benefit of a pension, profit-sharing, stock bonus, or other plan established under section 401, 403, 408, 408A, 414, 457, or 501(c) of the Internal Revenue Code of 1986, that is sponsored by the employer of the debtor, or an affiliate, successor, or pre-

decessor of such employer--

(A) to the extent that the amounts withheld and collected are used solely for payments relating to a loan from a plan under section 408(b)(1) of the Employee Retirement Income Security Act of 1974 or is subject to section 72(p) of the Internal Revenue Code of 1986; or

(B) a loan from a thrift savings plan permitted under subchapter III of chapter 84 of title 5, that satisfies the requirements of section 8433(g) of such title;

but nothing in this paragraph may be construed to provide that any loan made under a governmental plan under section 414(d), or a contract or account under section 403(b), of the Internal Revenue Code of 1986 constitutes a claim or a debt under this title;

(20) under subsection (a), of any act to enforce any lien against or security interest in real property following entry of the order under subsection (d)(4) as to such real property in any prior case under this title, for a period of 2 years after the date of the entry of such an order, except that the debtor, in a subsequent case under this title, may move for relief from such order based upon changed circumstances or for other good cause shown, after notice and a hearing;

(21) under subsection (a), of any act to enforce any lien against or security interest in real property--

(A) if the debtor is ineligible under section 109(g) to be a debtor in a case under this title; or

(B) if the case under this title was filed in violation of a bankruptcy court order in a prior case under this title prohibiting the debtor from being a debtor in another case under this title;

(22) subject to subsection (l), under subsection (a)(3), of the continuation of any eviction, unlawful detainer action, or similar proceeding by a lessor against a debtor involving residential property in which the debtor resides as a tenant under a lease or rental agreement and with respect to which the lessor has obtained before the date of the filing of the bankruptcy petition, a judgment for possession of such property against the debtor;

(23) subject to subsection (m), under subsection (a)(3), of an eviction action that seeks possession of the residential property in which the debtor resides as a tenant under a lease or rental agreement based on endangerment of such property or the illegal use of controlled substances on such property, but only if the lessor files with the court, and serves upon the debtor, a certification under penalty of perjury that such an eviction action has been filed, or that the debtor, during the 30-day period preceding the date of the filing of the certification, has endangered property or illegally used or allowed to be used a controlled substance on the property;

(24) under subsection (a), of any transfer that is not avoidable under section 544 and that is not avoidable under section 549;

(25) under subsection (a), of--
(A) the commencement or continuation of an investigation or action by a securities self regulatory organization to enforce such organization's regulatory power;

(B) the enforcement of an order or decision, other than for monetary sanctions, obtained in an action by such securities self regulatory organization to enforce such organization's regulatory power; or

(C) any act taken by such securities self regulatory organization to delist, delete, or refuse to permit quotation of any stock that does not meet applicable regulatory requirements;

(26) under subsection (a), of the setoff under applicable nonbankruptcy law of an income tax refund, by a governmental unit, with respect to a taxable period that ended before the date of the order for relief against an income tax liability for a taxable period that also ended before the date of the order for relief, except that in any case in which the setoff of an income tax refund is not permitted under applicable nonbankruptcy law because of a pending action to determine the amount or legality of a tax liability, the governmental unit may hold the refund pending the resolution of the action, unless the court, on the motion of the trustee and after notice and a hearing, grants the taxing authority adequate protection (within the meaning of section 361) for the secured claim of such authority in the setoff under section 506(a);

(27) under subsection (a), of the setoff by a master netting agreement participant of a mutual debt and claim under or in connection with one or more master netting agreements or any contract or agreement subject to such agreements that constitutes the setoff of a claim against the debtor for any payment or other transfer of property due from the debtor under or in connection with such agreements or any contract or agreement subject to

such agreements against any payment due to the debtor from such master netting agreement participant under or in connection with such agreements or any contract or agreement subject to such agreements or against cash, securities, or other property held by, pledged to, under the control of, or due from such master netting agreement participant to margin, guarantee, secure, or settle such agreements or any contract or agreement subject to such agreements, to the extent that such participant is eligible to exercise such offset rights under paragraph (6), (7), or (17) for each individual contract covered by the master netting agreement in issue; and

(28) under subsection (a), of the exclusion by the Secretary of Health and Human Services of the debtor from participation in the medicare program or any other Federal health care program (as defined in section 1128B(f) of the Social Security Act pursuant to title XI or XVIII of such Act).

The provisions of paragraphs (12) and (13) of this subsection shall apply with respect to any such petition filed on or before December 31, 1989.

(c) Except as provided in subsections (d), (e), (f), and (h) of this section--

(1) the stay of an act against property of the estate under subsection (a) of this section continues until such property is no longer property of the estate;

(2) the stay of any other act under subsection (a) of this section continues until the earliest of--

(A) the time the case is closed;

(B) the time the case is dismissed; or

(C) if the case is a case under chapter 7 of this title concerning an individual or a case under chapter 9, 11, 12, or 13 of this title, the time a discharge is granted or denied;

(3) if a single or joint case is filed by or against debtor who is an individual in a case under chapter 7, 11, or 13, and if a single or joint case of the debtor was pending within the preceding 1-year period but was dismissed, other than a case refiled under a chapter other than chapter 7 after dismissal under section 707(b)--

(A) the stay under subsection (a) with respect to any action taken with respect to a debt or property securing such debt or with respect to any lease shall terminate with respect to the debtor on the 30th day after the filing of the later case;

(B) on the motion of a party in interest for continuation of the automatic stay and upon notice and a hearing, the court may extend the stay in particular cases as to any or all creditors (subject to such conditions or limitations as the court may then impose) after notice and a hearing completed before the expiration of the 30-day period only if the party in interest demonstrates that the filing of the later case is in good faith as to the creditors to be stayed; and

(C) for purposes of subparagraph (B), a case is presumptively filed not in good faith (but such presumption may be rebutted by clear and convincing evidence to the contrary)--

(i) as to all creditors, if--

(I) more than 1 previous case under any of chapters 7, 11, and 13 in which the individual was a debtor was pending within the preceding 1-year period;

(II) a previous case under any of chapters 7, 11, and 13 in which the individual was a debtor was dismissed within such 1-year period, after the debtor failed to--

(aa) file or amend the petition or other documents as required by this title or the court without substantial excuse (but mere inadvertence or negligence shall not be a substantial excuse unless the dismissal was caused by the negligence of the debtor's attorney);

(bb) provide adequate protection as ordered by the court; or

(cc) perform the terms of a plan confirmed by the court; or

(III) there has not been a substantial change in the financial or personal affairs of the debtor since the dismissal of the next most previous case under chapter 7, 11, or 13 or any other reason to conclude that the later case will be concluded--

(aa) if a case under chapter 7, with a discharge; or

(bb) if a case under chapter 11 or 13, with a confirmed plan that will be fully performed; and

(ii) as to any creditor that commenced an action under subsection (d) in a previous case in which the individual was a debtor if, as of the date of dismissal of such case, that action was still pending or had been resolved by terminating, conditioning, or limiting the stay as to actions of such creditor; and

(4)

(A)

(i) if a single or joint case is filed by or against a debtor who is an individual under this title, and if 2 or more single or joint cases of the debtor were pending within the previous year but were dismissed, other than a case refiled under section 707(b), the stay under subsection (a) shall not go into effect upon the filing of the later case; and

(ii) on request of a party in interest, the court shall promptly enter an order confirming that no stay is in effect;

(B) if, within 30 days after the filing of the later case, a party in interest requests the court may order the stay to take effect in the case as to any or all creditors (subject to such conditions or limitations as the court may impose), after notice and a hearing, only if the party in interest demonstrates that the filing of the later case is in good faith as to the creditors to be stayed;

(C) a stay imposed under subparagraph (B) shall be effective on the date of the entry of the order allowing the stay to go into effect; and

(D) for purposes of subparagraph (B), a case is presumptively filed not in good faith (but such presumption may be rebutted by clear and convincing evidence to the contrary)--

(i) as to all creditors if--

(I) 2 or more previous cases under this title in which the individual was a debtor were pending within the 1-year period;

(II) a previous case under this title in which the individual was a debtor was dismissed within the time period stated in this paragraph after the debtor failed to file or amend the petition or other documents as required by this title or the court without substantial excuse (but mere inadvertence or negligence shall not be substantial excuse unless the dismissal was caused by the negligence of the debtor's attorney), failed to provide adequate protection as ordered by the court, or failed to perform the terms of a plan confirmed by the court; or

(III) there has not been a substantial change in the financial or personal affairs of the debtor since the dismissal of the next most previous case under this title, or any other reason to conclude that the later case will not be concluded, if a case under chapter 7, with a discharge, and if a case under chapter 11 or 13, with a confirmed plan that will be fully performed; or

(ii) as to any creditor that commenced an action under subsection (d) in a previous case in which the individual was a debtor if, as of the date of dismissal of such case, such action was still pending or had been resolved by terminating, conditioning, or limiting the stay as to such action of such creditor.

(d) On request of a party in interest and after notice and a hearing, the court shall grant relief from the stay provided under subsection (a) of this section, such as by terminating, annulling, modifying, or conditioning such stay--

(1) for cause, including the lack of adequate protection of an interest in property of such party in interest;

(2) with respect to a stay of an act against property under subsection (a) of this section, if--
(A) the debtor does not have an equity in such property; and
(B) such property is not necessary to an effective reorganization;

(3) with respect to a stay of an act against single asset real estate under subsection (a), by a creditor whose claim is secured by an interest in such real estate, unless, not later than the date that is 90 days after the entry of the order for relief (or such later date as the court may determine for cause by order entered within that 90-day period) or 30 days after the court determines that the debtor is subject to this paragraph, whichever is later--
(A) the debtor has filed a plan of reorganization that has a reasonable possibility of being confirmed within a reasonable time; or
(B) the debtor has commenced monthly payments that--
(i) may, in the debtor's sole discretion, notwithstanding section

363(c)(2), be made from rents or other income generated before, on, or after the date of the commencement of the case by or from the property to each creditor whose claim is secured by such real estate (other than a claim secured by a judgment lien or by an unmatured statutory lien); and

(ii) are in an amount equal to interest at the then applicable nondefault contract rate of interest on the value of the creditor's interest in the real estate; or

(4) with respect to a stay of an act against real property under subsection (a), by a creditor whose claim is secured by an interest in such real property, if the court finds that the filing of the petition was part of a scheme to delay, hinder, and defraud creditors that involved either--

(A) transfer of all or part ownership of, or other interest in, such real property without the consent of the secured creditor or court approval; or

(B) multiple bankruptcy filings affecting such real property.

If recorded in compliance with applicable State laws governing notices of interests or liens in real property, an order entered under paragraph (4) shall be binding in any other case under this title purporting to affect such real property filed not later than 2 years after the date of the entry of such order by the court, except that a debtor in a subsequent case under this title may move for relief from such order based upon changed circumstances or for good cause shown, after notice and a hearing. Any Federal, State, or local governmental unit that accepts notices of interests or liens in real property shall accept any certified copy of an order described in this subsection for indexing and recording.

(e)

(1) Thirty days after a request under subsection (d) of this section for relief from the stay of any act against property of the estate under subsection (a) of this section, such stay is terminated with respect to the party in interest making such request, unless the court, after notice and a hearing, orders such stay continued in effect pending the conclusion of, or as a result of, a final hearing and determination under subsection (d) of this section. A hearing under this subsection may be a preliminary hearing, or may be consolidated with the final hearing under subsection (d) of this section. The court shall order such stay continued in effect pending the conclusion of the final hearing under subsection (d) of this section if there is a reasonable likelihood that the party opposing relief from such stay will prevail at the conclusion of such final hearing. If the hearing under this subsection is a preliminary hearing, then such final hearing shall be concluded not later than thirty days after the conclusion of such preliminary hearing, unless the 30-day period is extended with the consent of the parties in interest or for a specific time which the court finds is required by compelling circumstances.

(2) Notwithstanding paragraph (1), in a case under chapter 7, 11, or 13 in which the debtor is an individual, the stay under subsection (a) shall terminate on the date that is 60 days after a request is made by a party in interest under subsection (d), unless--
(A) a final decision is rendered by the court during the 60-day period beginning on the date of the request; or
(B) such 60-day period is extended--
(i) by agreement of all parties in interest; or

(ii) by the court for such specific period of time as the court finds is required for good cause, as described in findings made by the court.

(f) Upon request of a party in interest, the court, with or without a hearing, shall grant such relief from the stay provided under subsection (a) of this section as is necessary to prevent irreparable damage to the interest of an entity in property, if such interest will suffer such damage before there is an opportunity for notice and a hearing under subsection (d) or (e) of this section.

(g) In any hearing under subsection (d) or (e) of this section concerning relief from the stay of any act under subsection (a) of this section--

(1) the party requesting such relief has the burden of proof on the issue of the debtor's equity in property; and

(2) the party opposing such relief has the burden of proof on all other issues.

(h)
(1) In a case in which the debtor is an individual, the stay provided by subsection (a) is terminated with respect to personal property of the estate or of the debtor securing in whole or in part a claim, or subject to an unexpired lease, and such personal property shall no longer be property of the estate if the debtor fails within the applicable time set by section 521(a)(2)--
(A) to file timely any statement of intention required under section 521(a)(2) with respect to such personal property or to indi-

cate in such statement that the debtor will either surrender such personal property or retain it and, if retaining such personal property, either redeem such personal property pursuant to section 722, enter into an agreement of the kind specified in section 524(c) applicable to the debt secured by such personal property, or assume such unexpired lease pursuant to section 365(p) if the trustee does not do so, as applicable; and

(B) to take timely the action specified in such statement, as it may be amended before expiration of the period for taking action, unless such statement specifies the debtor's intention to reaffirm such debt on the original contract terms and the creditor refuses to agree to the reaffirmation on such terms.

(2) Paragraph (1) does not apply if the court determines, on the motion of the trustee filed before the expiration of the applicable time set by section 521(a)(2), after notice and a hearing, that such personal property is of consequential value or benefit to the estate, and orders appropriate adequate protection of the creditor's interest, and orders the debtor to deliver any collateral in the debtor's possession to the trustee. If the court does not so determine, the stay provided by subsection (a) shall terminate upon the conclusion of the hearing on the motion.

(i) If a case commenced under chapter 7, 11, or 13 is dismissed due to the creation of a debt repayment plan, for purposes of subsection (c)(3), any subsequent case commenced by the debtor under any such chapter shall not be presumed to be filed not in good faith.

(j) On request of a party in interest, the court shall issue an order under subsection (c) confirming that the automatic stay has been terminated.

(k)

(1) Except as provided in paragraph (2), an individual injured by any willful violation of a stay provided by this section shall recover actual damages, including costs and attorneys' fees, and, in appropriate circumstances, may recover punitive damages.

(2) If such violation is based on an action taken by an entity in the good faith belief that subsection (h) applies to the debtor, the recovery under paragraph (1) of this subsection against such entity shall be limited to actual damages.

(l)

(1) Except as otherwise provided in this subsection, subsection (b)(22) shall apply on the date that is 30 days after the date on which the bankruptcy petition is filed, if the debtor files with the petition and serves upon the lessor a certification under penalty of perjury that--
(A) under nonbankruptcy law applicable in the jurisdiction, there are circumstances under which the debtor would be permitted to cure the entire monetary default that gave rise to the judgment for possession, after that judgment for possession was entered; and
(B) the debtor (or an adult dependent of the debtor) has deposited with the clerk of the court, any rent that would become due during the 30-day period after the filing of the bankruptcy petition.

(2) If, within the 30-day period after the filing of the bankruptcy petition, the debtor (or an adult dependent of the debtor) complies with paragraph (1) and files with the court and serves upon the lessor a further certification under penalty of perjury that the debtor (or an adult dependent of the debtor) has cured, under nonbankrupcty law applicable in the jurisdiction, the entire monetary default that gave rise to the judgment under which possession is sought by the lessor, subsection (b)(22) shall not apply, unless ordered to apply by the court under paragraph (3).

(3)
(A) If the lessor files an objection to any certification filed by the debtor under paragraph (1) or (2), and serves such objection upon the debtor, the court shall hold a hearing within 10 days after the filing and service of such objection to determine if the certification filed by the debtor under paragraph (1) or (2) is true.
(B) If the court upholds the objection of the lessor filed under subparagraph (A)--
(i) subsection (b)(22) shall apply immediately and relief from the stay provided under subsection (a)(3) shall not be required to enable the lessor to complete the process to recover full possession of the property; and
(ii) the clerk of the court shall immediately serve upon the lessor and the debtor a certified copy of the court's order upholding the lessor's objection.

(4) If a debtor, in accordance with paragraph (5), indicates on the petition that there was a judgment for possession of the resi-

dential rental property in which the debtor resides and does not file a certification under paragraph (1) or (2)--

(A) subsection (b)(22) shall apply immediately upon failure to file such certification, and relief from the stay provided under subsection (a)(3) shall not be required to enable the lessor to complete the process to recover full possession of the property; and

(B) the clerk of the court shall immediately serve upon the lessor and the debtor a certified copy of the docket indicating the absence of a filed certification and the applicability of the exception to the stay under subsection (b)(22).

(5)

(A) Where a judgment for possession of residential property in which the debtor resides as a tenant under a lease or rental agreement has been obtained by the lessor, the debtor shall so indicate on the bankruptcy petition and shall provide the name and address of the lessor that obtained that pre-petition judgment on the petition and on any certification filed under this subsection.

(B) The form of certification filed with the petition, as specified in this subsection, shall provide for the debtor to certify, and the debtor shall certify--

(i) whether a judgment for possession of residential rental housing in which the debtor resides has been obtained against the debtor before the date of the filing of the petition; and

(ii) whether the debtor is claiming under paragraph (1) that under nonbankruptcy law applicable in the jurisdiction, there are circumstances under which the debtor would be permitted to cure the entire monetary default that gave rise to the judgment for possession, after that judgment of possession was entered, and has made the appropriate deposit with the court.

(C) The standard forms (electronic and otherwise) used in a bankruptcy proceeding shall be amended to reflect the requirements of this subsection.

(D) The clerk of the court shall arrange for the prompt transmittal of the rent deposited in accordance with paragraph (1)(B) to the lessor.

(m)

(1) Except as otherwise provided in this subsection, subsection (b)(23) shall apply on the date that is 15 days after the date on which the lessor files and serves a certification described in subsection (b)(23).

(2)

(A) If the debtor files with the court an objection to the truth or legal sufficiency of the certification described in subsection (b)(23) and serves such objection upon the lessor, subsection (b)(23) shall not apply, unless ordered to apply by the court under this subsection.

(B) If the debtor files and serves the objection under subparagraph (A), the court shall hold a hearing within 10 days after the filing and service of such objection to determine if the situation giving rise to the lessor's certification under paragraph (1) existed or has been remedied.

(C) If the debtor can demonstrate to the satisfaction of the court that the situation giving rise to the lessor's certification under paragraph (1) did not exist or has been remedied, the stay provided under subsection (a)(3) shall remain in effect until the termination of the stay under this section.

(D) If the debtor cannot demonstrate to the satisfaction of the court that the situation giving rise to the lessor's certification under paragraph (1) did not exist or has been remedied--

(i) relief from the stay provided under subsection (a)(3) shall not be required to enable the lessor to proceed with the eviction; and

(ii) the clerk of the court shall immediately serve upon the lessor and the debtor a certified copy of the court's order upholding the lessor's certification.

(3) If the debtor fails to file, within 15 days, an objection under paragraph (2)(A)--

(A) subsection (b)(23) shall apply immediately upon such failure and relief from the stay provided under subsection (a)(3) shall not be required to enable the lessor to complete the process to recover full possession of the property; and

(B) the clerk of the court shall immediately serve upon the lessor and the debtor a certified copy of the docket indicating such failure.

(n)

(1) Except as provided in paragraph (2), subsection (a) does not apply in a case in which the debtor--

(A) is a debtor in a small business case pending at the time the petition is filed;

(B) was a debtor in a small business case that was dismissed for any reason by an order that became final in the 2-year period ending on the date of the order for relief entered with respect to the petition;

(C) was a debtor in a small business case in which a plan was confirmed in the 2-year period ending on the date of the order for relief entered with respect to the petition; or

(D) is an entity that has acquired substantially all of the assets or business of a small business debtor described in subparagraph (A), (B), or (C), unless such entity establishes by a preponderance of the evidence that such entity acquired substantially all of the assets or business of such small business debtor in good faith and not for the purpose of evading this paragraph.

(2) Paragraph (1) does not apply--

(A) to an involuntary case involving no collusion by the debtor with creditors; or

(B) to the filing of a petition if--

(i) the debtor proves by a preponderance of the evidence that the filing of the petition resulted from circumstances beyond the control of the debtor not foreseeable at the time the case then pending was filed; and

(ii) it is more likely than not that the court will confirm a feasible plan, but not a liquidating plan, within a reasonable period of time.

(o) The exercise of rights not subject to the stay arising under subsection (a) pursuant to paragraph (6), (7), (17), or (27) of subsection (b) shall not be stayed by any order of a court or administrative agency in any proceeding under this title.

APPENDIX C:
MEANS TEST FORM B-22A*

B 22A (Official Form 22A) (Chapter 7) (12/10)

In re _____
　　　　　　Debtor(s)

Case Number: _____
　　　　　　(If known)

According to the information required to be entered on this statement (check one box as directed in Part I, III, or VI of this statement):
☐ **The presumption arises.**
☐ **The presumption does not arise.**
☐ **The presumption is temporarily inapplicable.**

CHAPTER 7 STATEMENT OF CURRENT MONTHLY INCOME
AND MEANS-TEST CALCULATION

In addition to Schedules I and J, this statement must be completed by every individual chapter 7 debtor. If none of the exclusions in Part I applies, joint debtors may complete one statement only. If any of the exclusions in Part I applies, joint debtors should complete separate statements if they believe this is required by § 707(b)(2)(C).

	Part I. MILITARY AND NON-CONSUMER DEBTORS
1A	**Disabled Veterans.** If you are a disabled veteran described in the Declaration in this Part IA, (1) check the box at the beginning of the Declaration, (2) check the box for "The presumption does not arise" at the top of this statement, and (3) complete the verification in Part VIII. Do not complete any of the remaining parts of this statement. ☐ **Declaration of Disabled Veteran.** By checking this box, I declare under penalty of perjury that I am a disabled veteran (as defined in 38 U.S.C. § 3741(1)) whose indebtedness occurred primarily during a period in which I was on active duty (as defined in 10 U.S.C. § 101(d)(1)) or while I was performing a homeland defense activity (as defined in 32 U.S.C. §901(1)).
1B	**Non-consumer Debtors.** If your debts are not primarily consumer debts, check the box below and complete the verification in Part VIII. Do not complete any of the remaining parts of this statement. ☐ **Declaration of non-consumer debts.** By checking this box, I declare that my debts are not primarily consumer debts.
1C	**Reservists and National Guard Members; active duty or homeland defense activity.** Members of a reserve component of the Armed Forces and members of the National Guard who were called to active duty (as defined in 10 U.S.C. § 101(d)(1)) after September 11, 2001, for a period of at least 90 days, or who have performed homeland defense activity (as defined in 32 U.S.C. § 901(1)) for a period of at least 90 days, are excluded from all forms of means testing during the time of active duty or homeland defense activity and for 540 days thereafter (the "exclusion period"). If you qualify for this temporary exclusion, (1) check the appropriate boxes and complete any required information in the Declaration of Reservists and National Guard Members below, (2) check the box for "The presumption is temporarily inapplicable" at the top of this statement, and (3) complete the verification in Part VIII. **During your exclusion period you are not required to complete the balance of this form, but you must complete the form no later than 14 days after the date on which your exclusion period ends, unless the time for filing a motion raising the means test presumption expires in your case before your exclusion period ends.** ☐ **Declaration of Reservists and National Guard Members.** By checking this box and making the appropriate entries below, I declare that I am eligible for a temporary exclusion from means testing because, as a member of a reserve component of the Armed Forces or the National Guard a. ☐ I was called to active duty after September 11, 2001, for a period of at least 90 days and ☐ I remain on active duty /or/ ☐ I was released from active duty on _____, which is less than 540 days before this bankruptcy case was filed; OR b. ☐ I am performing homeland defense activity for a period of at least 90 days /or/ ☐ I performed homeland defense activity for a period of at least 90 days, terminating on _____, which is less than 540 days before this bankruptcy case was filed.

122   Jeffrey D. Holst

Part II. CALCULATION OF MONTHLY INCOME FOR § 707(b)(7) EXCLUSION		
2 Marital/filing status. Check the box that applies and complete the balance of this part of this statement as directed. a. ☐ Unmarried. **Complete only Column A ("Debtor's Income") for Lines 3-11.** b. ☐ Married, not filing jointly, with declaration of separate households. By checking this box, debtor declares under penalty of perjury: "My spouse and I are legally separated under applicable non-bankruptcy law or my spouse and I are living apart other than for the purpose of evading the requirements of § 707(b)(2)(A) of the Bankruptcy Code." **Complete only Column A ("Debtor's Income") for Lines 3-11.** c. ☐ Married, not filing jointly, without the declaration of separate households set out in Line 2.b above. **Complete both Column A ("Debtor's Income") and Column B ("Spouse's Income") for Lines 3-11.** d. ☐ Married, filing jointly. **Complete both Column A ("Debtor's Income") and Column B ("Spouse's Income") for Lines 3-11.**		
All figures must reflect average monthly income received from all sources, derived during the six calendar months prior to filing the bankruptcy case, ending on the last day of the month before the filing. If the amount of monthly income varied during the six months, you must divide the six-month total by six, and enter the result on the appropriate line.	**Column A** Debtor's Income	**Column B** Spouse's Income
3 Gross wages, salary, tips, bonuses, overtime, commissions.	$	$
4 Income from the operation of a business, profession or farm. Subtract Line b from Line a and enter the difference in the appropriate column(s) of Line 4. If you operate more than one business, profession or farm, enter aggregate numbers and provide details on an attachment. Do not enter a number less than zero. **Do not include any part of the business expenses entered on Line b as a deduction in Part V.** a. Gross receipts $ b. Ordinary and necessary business expenses $ c. Business income Subtract Line b from Line a	$	$
5 Rent and other real property income. Subtract Line b from Line a and enter the difference in the appropriate column(s) of Line 5. Do not enter a number less than zero. **Do not include any part of the operating expenses entered on Line b as a deduction in Part V.** a. Gross receipts $ b. Ordinary and necessary operating expenses $ c. Rent and other real property income Subtract Line b from Line a	$	$
6 Interest, dividends and royalties.	$	$
7 Pension and retirement income.	$	$
8 Any amounts paid by another person or entity, on a regular basis, for the household expenses of the debtor or the debtor's dependents, including child support paid for that purpose. Do not include alimony or separate maintenance payments or amounts paid by your spouse if Column B is completed. Each regular payment should be reported in only one column; if a payment is listed in Column A, do not report that payment in Column B.	$	$
9 Unemployment compensation. Enter the amount in the appropriate column(s) of Line 9. However, if you contend that unemployment compensation received by you or your spouse was a benefit under the Social Security Act, do not list the amount of such compensation in Column A or B, but instead state the amount in the space below: Unemployment compensation claimed to be a benefit under the Social Security Act Debtor $ _____ Spouse $ _____	$	$

B 22A (Official Form 22A) (Chapter 7) (12/10)   3

10	**Income from all other sources.** Specify source and amount. If necessary, list additional sources on a separate page. **Do not include alimony or separate maintenance payments paid by your spouse if Column B is completed, but include all other payments of alimony or separate maintenance.** Do not include any benefits received under the Social Security Act or payments received as a victim of a war crime, crime against humanity, or as a victim of international or domestic terrorism.		
	a. $		
	b. $		
	Total and enter on Line 10	$	$
11	**Subtotal of Current Monthly Income for § 707(b)(7).** Add Lines 3 thru 10 in Column A, and, if Column B is completed, add Lines 3 through 10 in Column B. Enter the total(s).	$	$
12	**Total Current Monthly Income for § 707(b)(7).** If Column B has been completed, add Line 11, Column A to Line 11, Column B, and enter the total. If Column B has not been completed, enter the amount from Line 11, Column A.	$	

Part III. APPLICATION OF § 707(b)(7) EXCLUSION

13	**Annualized Current Monthly Income for § 707(b)(7).** Multiply the amount from Line 12 by the number 12 and enter the result.	$
14	**Applicable median family income.** Enter the median family income for the applicable state and household size. (This information is available by family size at www.usdoj.gov/ust/ or from the clerk of the bankruptcy court.)	$
	a. Enter debtor's state of residence: _____ b. Enter debtor's household size: _____	
15	**Application of Section 707(b)(7).** Check the applicable box and proceed as directed. ☐ **The amount on Line 13 is less than or equal to the amount on Line 14.** Check the box for "The presumption does not arise" at the top of page 1 of this statement, and complete Part VIII; do not complete Parts IV, V, VI or VII. ☐ **The amount on Line 13 is more than the amount on Line 14.** Complete the remaining parts of this statement.	

Complete Parts IV, V, VI, and VII of this statement only if required. (See Line 15.)

	Part IV. CALCULATION OF CURRENT MONTHLY INCOME FOR § 707(b)(2)	
16	**Enter the amount from Line 12.**	$
17	**Marital adjustment.** If you checked the box at Line 2.c, enter on Line 17 the total of any income listed in Line 11, Column B that was NOT paid on a regular basis for the household expenses of the debtor or the debtor's dependents. Specify in the lines below the basis for excluding the Column B income (such as payment of the spouse's tax liability or the spouse's support of persons other than the debtor or the debtor's dependents) and the amount of income devoted to each purpose. If necessary, list additional adjustments on a separate page. If you did not check box at Line 2.c, enter zero.	
	a. $	
	b. $	
	c. $	
	Total and enter on Line 17.	$
18	**Current monthly income for § 707(b)(2).** Subtract Line 17 from Line 16 and enter the result.	$

Part V. CALCULATION OF DEDUCTIONS FROM INCOME

Subpart A: Deductions under Standards of the Internal Revenue Service (IRS)

19A	**National Standards: food, clothing and other items.** Enter in Line 19A the "Total" amount from IRS National Standards for Food, Clothing and Other Items for the applicable number of persons. (This information is available at www.usdoj.gov/ust/ or from the clerk of the bankruptcy court.) The applicable number of persons is the number that would currently be allowed as exemptions on your federal income tax return, plus the number of any additional dependents whom you support.	$
19B	**National Standards: health care.** Enter in Line a1 below the amount from IRS National Standards for Out-of-Pocket Health Care for persons under 65 years of age, and in Line a2 the IRS National Standards for Out-of-Pocket Health Care for persons 65 years of age or older. (This information is available at www.usdoj.gov/ust/ or from the clerk of the bankruptcy court.) Enter in Line b1 the applicable number of persons who are under 65 years of age, and enter in Line b2 the applicable number of persons who are 65 years of age or older. (The applicable number of persons in each age category is the number in that category that would currently be allowed as exemptions on your federal income tax return, plus the number of any additional dependents whom you support.) Multiply Line a1 by Line b1 to obtain a total amount for persons under 65, and enter the result in Line c1. Multiply Line a2 by Line b2 to obtain a total amount for persons 65 and older, and enter the result in Line c2. Add Lines c1 and c2 to obtain a total health care amount, and enter the result in Line 19B.	

Persons under 65 years of age		Persons 65 years of age or older		
a1.	Allowance per person	a2.	Allowance per person	
b1.	Number of persons	b2.	Number of persons	
c1	Subtotal	c2.	Subtotal	$

20A	**Local Standards: housing and utilities; non-mortgage expenses.** Enter the amount of the IRS Housing and Utilities Standards; non-mortgage expenses for the applicable county and family size. (This information is available at www.usdoj.gov/ust/ or from the clerk of the bankruptcy court). The applicable family size consists of the number that would currently be allowed as exemptions on your federal income tax return, plus the number of any additional dependents whom you support.	$
20B	**Local Standards: housing and utilities; mortgage/rent expense.** Enter, in Line a below, the amount of the IRS Housing and Utilities Standards; mortgage/rent expense for your county and family size (this information is available at www.usdoj.gov/ust/ or from the clerk of the bankruptcy court) (the applicable family size consists of the number that would currently be allowed as exemptions on your federal income tax return, plus the number of any additional dependents whom you support); enter on Line b the total of the Average Monthly Payments for any debts secured by your home, as stated in Line 42; subtract Line b from Line a and enter the result in Line 20B. **Do not enter an amount less than zero.**	

a.	IRS Housing and Utilities Standards; mortgage/rental expense	$	
b.	Average Monthly Payment for any debts secured by your home, if any, as stated in Line 42	$	
c.	Net mortgage/rental expense	Subtract Line b from Line a.	$

21	**Local Standards: housing and utilities; adjustment.** If you contend that the process set out in Lines 20A and 20B does not accurately compute the allowance to which you are entitled under the IRS Housing and Utilities Standards, enter any additional amount to which you contend you are entitled, and state the basis for your contention in the space below:	$

B 22A (Official Form 22A) (Chapter 7) (12/10)   6

29	**Other Necessary Expenses: education for employment or for a physically or mentally challenged child.** Enter the total average monthly amount that you actually expend for education that is a condition of employment and for education that is required for a physically or mentally challenged dependent child for whom no public education providing similar services is available.	$
30	**Other Necessary Expenses: childcare.** Enter the total average monthly amount that you actually expend on childcare—such as baby-sitting, day care, nursery and preschool. **Do not include other educational payments.**	$
31	**Other Necessary Expenses: health care.** Enter the total average monthly amount that you actually expend on health care that is required for the health and welfare of yourself or your dependents, that is not reimbursed by insurance or paid by a health savings account, and that is in excess of the amount entered in Line 19B. **Do not include payments for health insurance or health savings accounts listed in Line 34.**	$
32	**Other Necessary Expenses: telecommunication services.** Enter the total average monthly amount that you actually pay for telecommunication services other than your basic home telephone and cell phone service—such as pagers, call waiting, caller id, special long distance, or internet service—to the extent necessary for your health and welfare or that of your dependents. **Do not include any amount previously deducted.**	$
33	**Total Expenses Allowed under IRS Standards.** Enter the total of Lines 19 through 32.	$

Subpart B: Additional Living Expense Deductions
Note: Do not include any expenses that you have listed in Lines 19-32

34	**Health Insurance, Disability Insurance, and Health Savings Account Expenses.** List the monthly expenses in the categories set out in lines a-c below that are reasonably necessary for yourself, your spouse, or your dependents. <table><tr><td>a.</td><td>Health Insurance</td><td>$</td></tr><tr><td>b.</td><td>Disability Insurance</td><td>$</td></tr><tr><td>c.</td><td>Health Savings Account</td><td>$</td></tr></table> Total and enter on Line 34 **If you do not actually expend this total amount**, state your actual total average monthly expenditures in the space below: $ _____	$
35	**Continued contributions to the care of household or family members.** Enter the total average actual monthly expenses that you will continue to pay for the reasonable and necessary care and support of an elderly, chronically ill, or disabled member of your household or member of your immediate family who is unable to pay for such expenses.	$
36	**Protection against family violence.** Enter the total average reasonably necessary monthly expenses that you actually incurred to maintain the safety of your family under the Family Violence Prevention and Services Act or other applicable federal law. The nature of these expenses is required to be kept confidential by the court.	$
37	**Home energy costs.** Enter the total average monthly amount, in excess of the allowance specified by IRS Local Standards for Housing and Utilities, that you actually expend for home energy costs. **You must provide your case trustee with documentation of your actual expenses, and you must demonstrate that the additional amount claimed is reasonable and necessary.**	$
38	**Education expenses for dependent children less than 18.** Enter the total average monthly expenses that you actually incur, not to exceed $147.92* per child, for attendance at a private or public elementary or secondary school by your dependent children less than 18 years of age. **You must provide your case trustee with documentation of your actual expenses, and you must explain why the amount claimed is reasonable and necessary and not already accounted for in the IRS Standards.**	$

*Amount subject to adjustment on 4/01/13, and every three years thereafter with respect to cases commenced on or after the date of adjustment.

B 22A (Official Form 22A) (Chapter 7) (12/10)

29	**Other Necessary Expenses: education for employment or for a physically or mentally challenged child.** Enter the total average monthly amount that you actually expend for education that is a condition of employment and for education that is required for a physically or mentally challenged dependent child for whom no public education providing similar services is available.	$
30	**Other Necessary Expenses: childcare.** Enter the total average monthly amount that you actually expend on childcare—such as baby-sitting, day care, nursery and preschool. **Do not include other educational payments.**	$
31	**Other Necessary Expenses: health care.** Enter the total average monthly amount that you actually expend on health care that is required for the health and welfare of yourself or your dependents, that is not reimbursed by insurance or paid by a health savings account, and that is in excess of the amount entered in Line 19B. **Do not include payments for health insurance or health savings accounts listed in Line 34.**	$
32	**Other Necessary Expenses: telecommunication services.** Enter the total average monthly amount that you actually pay for telecommunication services other than your basic home telephone and cell phone service— such as pagers, call waiting, caller id, special long distance, or internet service—to the extent necessary for your health and welfare or that of your dependents. **Do not include any amount previously deducted.**	$
33	**Total Expenses Allowed under IRS Standards.** Enter the total of Lines 19 through 32.	$

Subpart B: Additional Living Expense Deductions
Note: Do not include any expenses that you have listed in Lines 19-32

34	**Health Insurance, Disability Insurance, and Health Savings Account Expenses.** List the monthly expenses in the categories set out in lines a-c below that are reasonably necessary for yourself, your spouse, or your dependents.	
	a. Health Insurance $	
	b. Disability Insurance $	
	c. Health Savings Account $	
	Total and enter on Line 34	$
	If you do not actually expend this total amount, state your actual total average monthly expenditures in the space below: $ _____	
35	**Continued contributions to the care of household or family members.** Enter the total average actual monthly expenses that you will continue to pay for the reasonable and necessary care and support of an elderly, chronically ill, or disabled member of your household or member of your immediate family who is unable to pay for such expenses.	$
36	**Protection against family violence.** Enter the total average reasonably necessary monthly expenses that you actually incurred to maintain the safety of your family under the Family Violence Prevention and Services Act or other applicable federal law. The nature of these expenses is required to be kept confidential by the court.	$
37	**Home energy costs.** Enter the total average monthly amount, in excess of the allowance specified by IRS Local Standards for Housing and Utilities, that you actually expend for home energy costs. **You must provide your case trustee with documentation of your actual expenses, and you must demonstrate that the additional amount claimed is reasonable and necessary.**	$
38	**Education expenses for dependent children less than 18.** Enter the total average monthly expenses that you actually incur, not to exceed $147.92* per child, for attendance at a private or public elementary or secondary school by your dependent children less than 18 years of age. **You must provide your case trustee with documentation of your actual expenses, and you must explain why the amount claimed is reasonable and necessary and not already accounted for in the IRS Standards.**	$

*Amount subject to adjustment on 4/01/13, and every three years thereafter with respect to cases commenced on or after the date of adjustment.

B 22A (Official Form 22A) (Chapter 7) (12/10)   7

39	**Additional food and clothing expense.** Enter the total average monthly amount by which your food and clothing expenses exceed the combined allowances for food and clothing (apparel and services) in the IRS National Standards, not to exceed 5% of those combined allowances. (This information is available at www.usdoj.gov/ust/ or from the clerk of the bankruptcy court.) **You must demonstrate that the additional amount claimed is reasonable and necessary.**				$
40	**Continued charitable contributions.** Enter the amount that you will continue to contribute in the form of cash or financial instruments to a charitable organization as defined in 26 U.S.C. § 170(c)(1)-(2).				$
41	**Total Additional Expense Deductions under § 707(b).** Enter the total of Lines 34 through 40				$

Subpart C: Deductions for Debt Payment

42	**Future payments on secured claims.** For each of your debts that is secured by an interest in property that you own, list the name of the creditor, identify the property securing the debt, state the Average Monthly Payment, and check whether the payment includes taxes or insurance. The Average Monthly Payment is the total of all amounts scheduled as contractually due to each Secured Creditor in the 60 months following the filing of the bankruptcy case, divided by 60. If necessary, list additional entries on a separate page. Enter the total of the Average Monthly Payments on Line 42.				

		Name of Creditor	Property Securing the Debt	Average Monthly Payment	Does payment include taxes or insurance?
	a.			$	☐ yes ☐ no
	b.			$	☐ yes ☐ no
	c.			$	☐ yes ☐ no
				Total: Add Lines a, b and c.	$

43	**Other payments on secured claims.** If any of debts listed in Line 42 are secured by your primary residence, a motor vehicle, or other property necessary for your support or the support of your dependents, you may include in your deduction 1/60th of any amount (the "cure amount") that you must pay the creditor in addition to the payments listed in Line 42, in order to maintain possession of the property. The cure amount would include any sums in default that must be paid in order to avoid repossession or foreclosure. List and total any such amounts in the following chart. If necessary, list additional entries on a separate page.

		Name of Creditor	Property Securing the Debt	1/60th of the Cure Amount
	a.			$
	b.			$
	c.			$
			Total: Add Lines a, b and c	$

44	**Payments on prepetition priority claims.** Enter the total amount, divided by 60, of all priority claims, such as priority tax, child support and alimony claims, for which you were liable at the time of your bankruptcy filing. **Do not include current obligations, such as those set out in Line 28.**	$

45	**Chapter 13 administrative expenses.** If you are eligible to file a case under chapter 13, complete the following chart, multiply the amount in line a by the amount in line b, and enter the resulting administrative expense.			
	a.	Projected average monthly chapter 13 plan payment.	$	
	b.	Current multiplier for your district as determined under schedules issued by the Executive Office for United States Trustees. (This information is available at www.usdoj.gov/ust/ or from the clerk of the bankruptcy court.)	x	
	c.	Average monthly administrative expense of chapter 13 case	Total: Multiply Lines a and b	$
46	**Total Deductions for Debt Payment.** Enter the total of Lines 42 through 45.			$

Subpart D: Total Deductions from Income

47	**Total of all deductions allowed under § 707(b)(2).** Enter the total of Lines 33, 41, and 46.	$

Part VI. DETERMINATION OF § 707(b)(2) PRESUMPTION

48	**Enter the amount from Line 18 (Current monthly income for § 707(b)(2))**	$
49	**Enter the amount from Line 47 (Total of all deductions allowed under § 707(b)(2))**	$
50	**Monthly disposable income under § 707(b)(2).** Subtract Line 49 from Line 48 and enter the result	$
51	**60-month disposable income under § 707(b)(2).** Multiply the amount in Line 50 by the number 60 and enter the result.	$
52	**Initial presumption determination.** Check the applicable box and proceed as directed. ☐ **The amount on Line 51 is less than $7,025*.** Check the box for "The presumption does not arise" at the top of page 1 of this statement, and complete the verification in Part VIII. Do not complete the remainder of Part VI. ☐ **The amount set forth on Line 51 is more than $11,725*.** Check the box for "The presumption arises" at the top of page 1 of this statement, and complete the verification in Part VIII. You may also complete Part VII. Do not complete the remainder of Part VI. ☐ **The amount on Line 51 is at least $7,025*, but not more than $11,725*.** Complete the remainder of Part VI (Lines 53 through 55).	
53	**Enter the amount of your total non-priority unsecured debt**	$
54	**Threshold debt payment amount.** Multiply the amount in Line 53 by the number 0.25 and enter the result.	$
55	**Secondary presumption determination.** Check the applicable box and proceed as directed. ☐ **The amount on Line 51 is less than the amount on Line 54.** Check the box for "The presumption does not arise" at the top of page 1 of this statement, and complete the verification in Part VIII. ☐ **The amount on Line 51 is equal to or greater than the amount on Line 54.** Check the box for "The presumption arises" at the top of page 1 of this statement, and complete the verification in Part VIII. You may also complete Part VII.	

Part VII: ADDITIONAL EXPENSE CLAIMS

56	**Other Expenses.** List and describe any monthly expenses, not otherwise stated in this form, that are required for the health and welfare of you and your family and that you contend should be an additional deduction from your current monthly income under § 707(b)(2)(A)(ii)(I). If necessary, list additional sources on a separate page. All figures should reflect your average monthly expense for each item. Total the expenses.		
		Expense Description	Monthly Amount
	a.		$
	b.		$
	c.		$
		Total: Add Lines a, b and c	$

Amounts are subject to adjustment on 4/01/13, and every three years thereafter with respect to cases commenced on or after the date of adjustment.

*Notice: this form has been shortened due to space considerations, all relevant sections appear. However in this state this form can not be filed with a Federal Bankruptcy Court. Please seek Professional advice before attempting to file for any form of bankruptcy protection.

APPENDIX D:
MEDIAN INCOMES BY STATE

These numbers are current as of November 10, 2011 keep in mind that these number are adjust periodically and it is always important to get current numbers before making an eligibility determination.

These numbers are published on the website for the Justice Department.

Add $7,500 for each individual in excess of 4.

State	Single Earner	2 People	3 People	4 People
		Family Size		
Alabama	$38,642	$46,900	$52,460	$64,016
Alaska	$51,950	$75,460	$81,447	$85,964
Arizona	$42,603	$55,404	$59,659	$67,113
Arkansas	$32,834	$44,081	$49,599	$54,401
California	$48,009	$62,970	$68,670	$78,869
Colorado	$48,598	$64,679	$70,861	$83,976
Connecticut	$57,863	$71,961	$83,655	$103,314
Delaware	$48,415	$62,432	$68,518	$85,305
District of Columbia	$48,822	$80,172	$80,172	$80,172
Florida	$40,029	$50,130	$54,594	$65,135
Georgia	$39,384	$52,024	$56,682	$69,239
Hawaii	$50,664	$64,179	$75,670	$86,587
Idaho	$39,050	$48,648	$55,453	$61,480
Illinois	$46,355	$60,073	$69,910	$81,097
Indiana	$40,135	$51,104	$59,028	$69,226
Iowa	$40,456	$56,036	$63,510	$75,569
Kansas	$41,654	$57,174	$64,863	$69,272

Kentucky	$37,606	$45,081	$51,883	$63,768
Louisiana	$38,108	$46,704	$55,699	$67,239
Maine	$39,497	$51,600	$59,050	$68,466
Maryland	$55,774	$74,493	$87,152	$103,361
Massachusetts	$55,049	$68,243	$83,736	$102,110
Michigan	$42,562	$50,738	$60,161	$71,758
Minnesota	$45,760	$61,690	$74,082	$85,146
Mississippi	$32,658	$41,579	$47,058	$55,711
Missouri	$39,332	$51,120	$58,610	$69,832
Montana	$38,577	$52,412	$56,265	$67,921
Nebraska	$38,915	$54,124	$65,486	$71,097
Nevada	$43,041	$57,541	$60,783	$70,509
New Hampshire	$51,460	$63,534	$82,465	$89,990
New Jersey	$59,060	$70,680	$85,573	$101,106
New Mexico	$37,274	$51,855	$52,303	$53,709
New York	$46,295	$57,777	$68,396	$83,942
North Carolina	$37,781	$50,630	$55,468	$67,578
North Dakota	$41,443	$56,411	$69,328	$79,637
Ohio	$40,749	$51,319	$60,247	$72,625
Oklahoma	$36,884	$49,711	$54,135	$64,037
Oregon	$44,707	$55,553	$60,523	$72,767
Pennsylvania	$44,897	$53,706	$67,113	$79,916
Rhode Island	$46,136	$58,511	$72,184	$88,593
South Carolina	$37,055	$50,500	$52,738	$63,074
South Dakota	$35,582	$53,443	$58,794	$68,016
Tennessee	$38,144	$47,194	$53,227	$63,217
Texas	$38,294	$55,178	$56,445	$65,477
Utah	$50,635	$56,126	$61,944	$69,834
Vermont	$43,042	$57,948	$65,829	$78,392
Virginia	$50,296	$63,613	$73,260	$86,990
Washington	$49,930	$63,224	$72,524	$82,602
West Virginia	$39,750	$42,607	$51,350	$60,280
Wisconsin	$41,150	$56,080	$66,256	$77,438
Wyoming	$46,172	$60,829	$69,677	$76,361

GLOSSARY TERMS

341 Meeting: Common name of the creditors meeting that takes place pursuant to §341 of the Bankruptcy Code.

Automatic stay: a type of injunction that stops all collection activities, lawsuits, foreclosures, garnishments; this injunction occurs at the moments the bankruptcy petition is filed.

Bankruptcy Estate: All interests of the debtor in property existing at the time the bankruptcy petition is filed. Property interests include tangible and intangible items and is not limited to items currently in possession or currently titled to debtor, it includes all equitable and legal interests, unless said property is exempted by the debtor pursuant to 11 USC §523.

Chapter 7: Most common type of bankruptcy available for business and for individuals. In most cases individuals who file this chapter can keep all of their assets and are not required to pay any of their debts, it is for this reason it is sometimes also referred to as "Total bankruptcy"

Chapter 9: A form of bankruptcy providing for the reorganization of municipalities such as cities, villages, school districts, taxing districts and counties.

Chapter 11: A reorganization proceeding in which the debtor may continue in business or in possession of its property, as a debtor in possession. A confirmed Chapter 11 plan sets the terms and the manner in which the claims of creditors will be paid.

Chapter 12: A reorganization plan for family farmers whose debts fall within prescribed limits.

Chapter 13: Is a type of bankruptcy only available to real people (businesses cannot file this type) It is a repayment plan bankruptcy that last between 3 years and 5 years, with the debtor typically paying monthly or weekly payments. At the conclusion of the 3-5 year period any remaining debt can be discharged.

Chapter 15: The chapter in the Bankruptcy Code dealing with cross-border insolvency issues

Confirmation: The bankruptcy Judge's official approval of a plan or reorganization in chapters 11, 12, or 13.

Conversion: The process by which a case is moved from one chapter of the code to another (i.e. by which a Chapter 7 is converted to a Chapter 13)

Current Monthly Income: The average monthly income received by the debtor over the six calendar months before commencement of the bankruptcy case, including regular contributions to household expenses from nondebtors and income from the debtor's spouse if the petition is a joint petition, but not including social security income and certain other payments made because the debtor is the victim of certain crimes. 11 U.S.C. § 101(10A).

Debtor: The person or entity who has filed for relief under the

Bankruptcy Code.

Discharge: The process by which the debtor's legal obligation to pay certain debts is removed. The discharge comes as an order from the court eliminating the legal obligation to pay the discharged debts.

Dismissal: The termination of a bankruptcy case without discharge, can result from fraud, abuse, or other violations of the code. The effect of dismissal is to eliminate the relief of bankruptcy following dismissal creditors are restored to their previous position regarding the debtor as if no bankruptcy were filed.

Equity: Remaining value in debtor's property after deducting the value of the allowable secured interests.

Exemptions: Lists of the kinds and values of certain types of property that are allowed to be excluded by the debtor from potential sale by the trustee. Exempt property is kept by the debtor free of the claims of trustee.

Insider: Any relative or partner of the debtor, or in the case of a debtor corporation any person in control of the corporation

Joint Petition: Bankruptcy petition filed by a husband and wife debtor.

Lien: An interest in property whether real or personal that secures a debt attached to that property. Liens create a right to take and hold or sell the property of the debtor for failure to pay or comply with the underlying obligation.

Liquidation: The sale of the non-exempt portion of the debtors property for the benefit of the debtors creditors.

Means Test: The means test was created as part of the Bankruptcy Reform and Protection Act of 2005. It is a test to determine the eligibility of the individual debtor (and debtor's joint filing spouse). It is an income and and expense based test that is used to prevent abuse of Chapter 7 of the Bankruptcy Code. Abuse is presumed if the debtor's aggregate current monthly income (see definition above) over 5 years, net of certain statutorily allowed expenses is more than (i) $10,950, or (ii) 25% of the debtor's non-priority unsecured debt, as long as that amount is at least $6,575. The debtor may rebut a presumption of abuse only by a showing of special circumstances that justify additional expenses or adjustments of current monthly income.

Nondischargeable Debt: Is a debt that cannot be eliminated in bankruptcy. These types of debts remain in force following the successful completion of a bankruptcy by the debtor.

Personal Property: All assets held by debtor that is not a form of real estate, includes cars, stocks and bonds and other non real holdings.

Preference: A debt payment made with in 90 days of the date of filing to a non insider or up to one year before before filing if it was to an insider.

Proof of claim: The form filed with the court establishing the creditor's claim against the debtor.

Property of the estate: All non exempt property is property of the bankruptcy estate. This property can be sold for the benefit of the creditors.

Reaffirmation: The process by which a debtor agrees to remain liable for an otherwise dischargeable debt. This can be used to allow the debtor to keep a secured asset such as a house or car.

Schedules: Detailed lists filed by the debtor along with the filing of the petition showing the debtor's assets, liabilities, and other financial information.

Statement of Financial Affairs: A series of questions that the debtor is required to answer in writing concerning their income history, their prior involvement in lawsuits, and any potentially preferential transfers of property that they have made.

Trustee: Court appointed official charged with overseeing the bankruptcy case and protecting the interests of the creditors.

ABOUT THE AUTHOR

Jeffrey D. Holst holds both a Bachelors of Science and Masters of Business Administration from Grand Valley State University and a Juris Doctorate from Michigan State University. Holst graduated early from law school, and with honors. While he was there he earned the jurisprudence award in individual income taxation. He was also selected as the graduating class speaker. As an attorney in the West Michigan area, Holst filed hundreds of bankruptcies, counseling individuals, families, and business owners about the process and about whether bankruptcy was the right choice for them.

He currently lives in Chattanooga Tennessee with his wife, Becky.